Bush Theatre

The Bush Theatre presents the world premiere of

FUCK THE POLAR BEARS

by Tanya Ronder

11 September – 24 October 2015

Bush Theatre, London

Fuck the Polar Bears

by Tanya Ronder

Cast

(in order of appearance)

Gordon	**Andrew Whipp**
Serena	**Susan Stanley**
Blundhilde	**Salóme R Gunnarsdóttir**
Clarence	**Jon Foster**
Rachel	**Bella Padden / Eléa Vicas**

Creative Team

Director	**Caroline Byrne**
Designer	**Chiara Stephenson**
Design Associate	**Nina Patel-Grainger**
Assistant Director	**Mark-Stuart Flynn**
Lighting Designer	**Tim Deiling**
Sound Designer	**Josh Anio Grigg**
Costume Designer	**Bex Kemp**
Movement Director	**Steffany George**
Voice and Singing Coach	**Hazel Holder**
Company Stage Manager	**Annette Waldie**
Assistant Stage Manager	**Lina Hallem**
Set Builder	**Ridiculous Solutions**
Construction of light frame	**Lighting Initiative**

The Bush would like to thank the Royal Court, Mrs Florist, Ridiculous Solutions, Lighting Initiative, System Sound & Light Ltd, Stage Solutions, Julie's Bicycle, and Tim Crouch.

The Bush Theatre is committed to promoting environmental sustainability in everything we do. To view our progress, please visit: bushtheatre.co.uk/environmental-sustainability

Cast and Crew

Andrew Whipp (Gordon)
Andrew's theatre credits include *Now This Is Not the End* (Arcola); *Farragut North* (Southwark Playhouse); *The Dark at the Top of the Stairs* (Belgrade Theatre); *Macbeth, King Lear* (Shakespeare's Globe); *Celebration, Arcadia* (Gate, Dublin); *Before the Flood* (Rough Cuts, Royal Court); *Much Ado about Nothing* (Stafford); *Best Men* (The Sticking Place); *The Misanthrope* (Bury St Edmonds); *The Child* (Gate); *Les Liaisons Dangereuses* (No.1 tour); *See How They Run* (Watermill); *King Lear, The Taming of the Shrew* (Ludlow).

Television credits include *Death in Paradise, A Song for Jenny, Holby City, EastEnders, Heartbeat, Doctors* (BBC); *Suspicion* (Discovery ID); *Critical* (Leftbank/Sky); *Spotless* (Tandem & Canal Plus); *Outlander* (Sony, Starz & Leftbank); *When Harvey Met Bob* (BBC/RTÉ); *Not Going Out* (Avalon/BBC); *City Lights* (ITV); *Love Lies Bleeding* (Granada); *Emmerdale, Heartbeat* (ITV).

Film includes *The Fourth Kind* and *Amazing Grace*.

Susan Stanley (Serena)
Susan trained at LAMDA. She most recently played the title role in *Portia Coughlan* (The Old Red Lion; nominated Best Female Performance, Offies 2015). Other theatre credits include *The Separation* (Theatre503); *Almost Maine* (Park); *The Separation* (Project Arts Centre, Dublin); *The Last Confessions of a Scallywag* (The Mill at Sonning) and *Bedbound* (The Lion and Unicorn).

Film credits include *Hotel Amenities* (Atraco Perfecto Productions; Best Actress, Malaga Film Festival, 2013); *Shadows in the Wind* (Atraco Perfecto Productions); *This Chair is Not Me, The End of the Nine Till Five* (dir. Andy Taylor Smith); *Timelarks* (dir. John Edwards) and *Resurrecting the Streetwalker* (Ozgur Uyanik).

Susan is Co-Founder of theatre company Pixilated.

Salóme R Gunnarsdóttir (Blundhilde)
Originally from Iceland, *Fuck the Polar Bears* marks Salóme's London theatre debut. Other theatre work includes *The Crucible, Spamalot, Assemblywomen* and *Óvitar*, all at the National Theatre of Iceland.

Film and television credits include *The Lava Field: Hraunið* (Pegasus Pictures); *Stelpurnar 5* (Saga Film); *Autumn Lights, Bakk* (Mystery Island); *Paris of the North* and *Megaphone* (Zik Zak Filmworks). She has most recently filmed the role of Toma in *Legends* for Fox 21.

Rachel (Bella Padden)
Bella is seven years old and has been dancing with Associates Dance School, Tonbridge, since she was two, taking part in national competitions and winning personality of the year out of 300 children. Theatre credits include *Cinderella* (Tunbridge Wells, forthcoming). Bella is represented by Alphabet Kidz.

Rachel (Eléa Vicas)
Eléa is eight years old and is a student at Stagecoach in Primrose Hill. She recently appeared as Alice in the film *The Prowler*, a psychological thriller written by author M. J. Arlidge, and has completed a short film with her younger brother to be shown on TV this Christmas. Eléa has also appeared in several commercials including KLM and Cheerios. Her hobbies include writing stories, drawing, yoga, singing and dancing.

Clarence (Jon Foster)
Jon's theatre work includes *buckets* (Orange Tree Theatre); *All I Want* (Jackson's Lane); *Idomeneus, Trojan Women, Dream Story, Mud* (Gate); *Cheese* (fanSHEN); *A Beginning, A Middle and An End, Tenet* (Greyscale); *Invisible* (Transport Theatre); *The Alchemist* (Firehouse Creative); *A New Way to Please You, Sejanus: His Fall, Speaking Like Magpies, Thomas More* (RSC); *How to Tell the Monsters from the Misfits* (Birmingham Rep); *Long Time Dead* (Paines Plough); *After Heggarty* (Finborough); *Food* (Traverse); *Dr Jekyll and Mr Hyde* (Babayaga); *Free From Sorrow* (Living Pictures); *Romeo and Juliet* (Creation); *Oliver Twist* (Instant Classics); *The Melancholy Hussar* (Etcetera); *The Two Gentlemen of Verona* (Pentameters) and *Treasure Island* (Palace Theatre).

Television credits include *Da Vinci's Demons, The Great Fire, New Tricks, Rev, The Smoke, Southcliffe, The Town, Mrs Biggs, Abroad, Come Rain Come Shine, EastEnders, Law and Order, The Bill, Clone, The IT Crowd, The Last Enemy, Instinct* and *Silent Witness*.

Films credits include *Nice Guy* and *Love's Kitchen*.

Tanya Ronder (Playwright)
Adaptations for theatre include *Dara* and *Liolà* (National Theatre); *Macbett* (RSC); *Filumena* and *Blood Wedding* (Almeida); *Peter Pan* (Kensington Gardens, 02 and USA tour); *Vernon God Little* (Olivier nomination for Best New Play, WhatsOnStage nomination for Best New Comedy) and *Peribanez* (Young Vic). Her first original play *Table* (National Theatre) opened the Shed to critical acclaim in 2013. Films include the short, *King Bastard* (dir. Rufus Norris). Tanya is currently developing a series for BBC, *Big Amy*, with co-writer Deborah Bruce.

Caroline Byrne (Director)
Caroline's directing credits include *Old Vic New Voices Festival* (Old Vic); *Electra* (Caird Studio, Cardiff); *Eclipsed* (Gate); *Gate 35 Gala* (Louise Blouin Foundation); *Leaving Home Party* (Farnham Maltings tour); *By Mr Farquhar* (UK City of Culture 2013); *Text Messages* (Project, Dublin); *Shakespeare in a Suitcase* (co-directed with Tim Crouch for RSC); *The Recovery Position* (Lion and Unicorn); *Twizzler Soaked Ecstasy* (devised, Bernhard Theatre Studio); *The Children* (Embassy Theatre) and *Attempts on her Life* (Durham Theatre, Berkeley, USA). As Assistant Director: *Adler and Gibb* (Royal Court); *Wendy and Peter Pan* (RSC) and *King Lear* (RSC tour). As Associate Director at the Gate Theatre (2014/15): *Grounded* and *Purple Heart*.

Chiara Stephenson (Designer)
Chiara worked at the Donmar Warehouse for Christopher Oram between 2008–2010 and is currently Associate Designer to Es Devlin. She is currently Associate Designer on *Hamlet* at the Barbican, Rio Opening Ceremony for the Olympics and *Freischutz* at Royal Danish Opera for Es Devlin.

As Associate Designer, credits include *The Nether* (Royal Court); *The Brit Awards 2015*; *America Psycho the Musical*, *Chimerica* (Almeida); *Miley Cyrus Bangerz* (world tour); *London 2012 Olympic Closing Ceremony*; *Kanye West and Jay Z Watch the Throne tour*; *Beatrice and Benedict* (Theatre an der Wien); *Cunning Little Vixen* (Royal Danish Opera); *Les Troyens* (ROH); *Master & Margarita* (Complicite); *Batman Live* (world tour); *Don Giovanni* (MET, New York); *Madame Butterfly*, Houston Grand Opera, *A Streetcar Named Desire*, *Hamlet*, *Madame De Sade* (Donmar Warehouse, Wyndam's season); *Sister Act the Musical* (Palladium) and *Hairspray* (European tour).

As Designer, credits include *Eclipsed* (Gate); *The Making of Don Giovanni* (exhibition design, ROH); *Miley Cyrus and Madonna* (MTV unplugged TV performance 2014); *All's Well That Ends Well* (Abigail Anderson, PMA Theatre, Liverpool); *Arcadia* (Unity Theatre, Liverpool) and *The Massacre* (Theatre Royal, Bury St Edmunds).

Nina Patel-Grainger (Design Associate)
Nina is Design Fellow at the Bush Theatre as part of the BBC Performing Arts Fellowship scheme 2015.

Since graduating from the Liverpool Institute of Performing Arts in 2010, Nina has worked as a freelance theatre designer and scenic artist for various companies around the UK including Liverpool Everyman, Birmingham REP, Slung Low and the RSC.

Current and forthcoming projects include *No Border* (written and directed by Carla Kingham) and *The H Word* (directed by Roy Alexander-Weise).

Mark-Stuart Flynn (Assistant Director)
Mark's theatre credits include *Antigone Reloaded* (Broadway Theatre); *Three Sisters* (Stratford Square); *Oliver* (Waterman's Theatre) and *DNA* (The Helix Theatre). As Assistant Director, credits include *Misanthropes* (Old Vic); *An Invitation from Me to You* (Tristan Bates Theatre) and *A Midsummer Night's Dream* (the Empty Space).

Tim Deiling (Lighting Designer)
Tim's credits include *American Idiot* (Arts Theatre); *Guys and Dolls* (Guildhall); *Dick Whittington* (Lyric Hammersmith); *Miracle on 34th Street* (UK tour); *HMS Pinafore* (Hackney Empire); *Incognito* (Bush); *The Dr Who Experience* (BBC); *Bare* (Greenwich); *Loserville the Musical, Whistle Down the Wind, Pacific Overtures, Bare, Billy* (The Union); *Good With People* (59E59, NYC); *The 8th* (Barbican); *Wigan, 65 Miles* (Hull Truck); *The Last Days of Judas Iscariot* (Platform Theatre); *Chips With Everything* (Embassy Studio); *As Is* (Finbourgh); *The Oikos Project, Protozoa* (The Red Room); *Zombie Prom the Musical* (Landor); *Macbeth* (Sprite Productions) and *Boiling Frogs* (Factory Theatre). Tim was Associate Lighting Designer for the National Theatre and has also worked as Assistant Lighting Designer on projects including *Scottsboro Boys, White Christmas* (West End); *Chicago the Musical* (UK tour, China, Madrid, Spanish tour, Seol Korea); *9 to 5 the Musical* (UK tour); *Pipin* (Chocolate Factory) and *High School Musical 2* (UK tour). Film work includes *Animal Charm, The Actress, Suzie Luvitt* (Ben Edwards) and *The Prank Show* (BBC). In 2008, Tim received Young Lighting Designer of the Year from the Association of Lighting Designers.

Josh Anio Grigg (Sound Designer)
Josh works mainly with sound design but also with other new media practices including video production and interactive software/hardware installations. He completed a Drama, Theatre and Performance degree at Roehampton University of Surrey in 2008. Josh has worked on productions in multiple venues in London, including the National Theatre, Jermyn Street Theatre and Yard Theatre. He also creates music and installations with artist Holly White collaboratively as Goth Tech.

Bex Kemp (Costume Designer)

Bex's design credits include *Pentecost* (RCSSD, Webber Douglas Studio/Derby LIVE); *Othello* (Greenwich/Underbelly Topside); *Becoming Mohammed* (The Space); *Interventionist* (Shunt, The Jetty); *About Miss Julie* (King's Head); *As You Like It* (UK tour); *Our Space* (Lost Theatre); *Variations on the Death of Trotsky* (RCSSD, PhD Research Performance); *Scenes from the Big Picture* (RCSSD, Embassy Theatre) and *The Common Chorus* (RCSSD, Webber Douglas).

As Supervisor: *The Water Palace* (Tête á Tête); *The Low Road* (RCSSD); *Citizen Puppet*, *Push* (New Diorama); *The Man of Mode*, *The Commune* and *The Good Person of Setzuan* (RCSSD).

As Design Assistant: *The Trial*, *The Government Inspector* (Young Vic); *The Boy Who Climbed Out of His Face* (Shunt, The Jetty); *Sleeping Beauty* (Salisbury Playhouse), *Chariots of Fire* (Hampstead); *Decade* (Headlong); *Carmen* (Salzburg Festival) and *The Duchess of Malfi* (Punchdrunk).

Bex studied at Central School of Speech and Drama graduating in 2012.

Steffany George (Movement Director)

Steffany George is currently Head of Movement at East 15 Acting School, Southend, on four distinct undergraduate courses: Physical Theatre, Acting and Stage Combat, World Performance, and Community Theatre. Movement Direction credits include *Eclipsed* (dir. Caroline Byrne, Gate Theatre) and *The Master and Margarita* (dir. Shane Dempsey). She hails from NYC where she taught and directed plays at The Stella Adler Studio of Acting from 1996–2006.

Hazel Holder (Voice and Singing Coach)

Hazel's theatre credits include *The Bakkhai* (Almeida); *As You Like It*, *Medea*, *Death and the King's Horseman* (National Theatre); *The Tempest* (RSC); *Dart's Love* (Tête à Tête Opera Festival); *Zero* (Clod Ensemble); *Six Characters in Search of an Author* (Headlong) and *The Bacchae* (National Theatre of Scotland and Lincoln Center, Broadway). Television includes *EastEnders* and *The Cambridge Spies*. Film includes *The Followed*. Radio includes *Something Understood* and *Death and the King's Horseman* (BBC R4 & R3). As Voice Coach: RADA, Arts Ed, Guildhall School of Music & Drama; *The Rolling Stone* (Royal Exchange, Manchester); *Eclipsed*, *The Rise & Shine of Comrade Fiasco* (Gate) and *The Initiate* (Paines Plough). Hazel is a member of a cappella groups The Shout and The Helen Chadwick Group. She also works with Marginal Voices, a charity that helps trafficked women dramatise their experiences.

" A powerhouse
of new writing"
– Sunday Times Culture

Bush Theatre

We make theatre for London. Now.

The Bush is a world-famous home for new plays and an internationally renowned champion of playwrights. We discover, nurture and produce the best new writers from the widest range of backgrounds from our home in a distinctive corner of west London.

The Bush has won over 100 awards and developed an enviable reputation for touring its acclaimed productions nationally and internationally.

We are excited by exceptional new voices, stories and perspectives – particularly those with contemporary bite which reflect the vibrancy of British culture now.

Now located in a recently renovated library building on the Uxbridge Road in the heart of Shepherd's Bush, the theatre houses a 144-seat auditorium, rehearsal rooms and a lively café bar.

bushtheatre.co.uk

Bush Theatre

THANK YOU TO OUR SUPPORTERS

The Bush Theatre would like to extend a very special thank you to the following Star Supporters, Corporate Members and Trusts & Foundations whose valuable contributions help us to nurture, develop and present some of the brightest new literary stars and theatre artists.

LONE STAR

Eric Abraham
Gianni Alen-Buckley
Michael Alen-Buckley
Rafael & Anne-Helene Biosse Duplan
Garvin & Steffanie Brown
Siri & Rob Cope
Alice Findlay
Aditya Mittal
Miles Morland
Lady Susie Sainsbury
James & Virginia Turnbull
Mr & Mrs Anthony Whyatt

HANDFUL OF STARS

Anonymous
Clive and Helena Butler
Clare Clark
Clyde Cooper
Simon & Katherine Johnson
Emmie Jones
Paul & Cathy Kafka
V & F Lukey
Vera Monotti Graziadei
Charlie & Polly McAndrew
Paige Nelson
Philip & Biddy Percival
Robert Rooney
Joana & Henrik Schliemann
Philippa Seal & Philip Jones QC
The Van Tulleken Family
Charlotte & Simon Warshaw

RISING STARS

ACT IV
Nicholas Alt
Anonymous
Melanie Aram
Tessa Bamford
Christopher Bevan
Charlie Bigham
David Brooks
Maggie Burrows
Simon Burstein
Matthew Byam Shaw
Jennifer Caruso Viall
Benedetta Cassinelli
Tim & Andrea Clark
Sarah Clarke
Claude & Susie Cochin de Billy
Carole & Neville Conrad
Susie Cuff
Matthew Cushen
Liz & Simon Dingemans
Andrew & Amanda Duncan
Charles Emmerson

RISING STARS CONTINUED

Catherine Faulks
Natalie Fellowes
Lady Antonia Fraser
Rosie & Richard Gledhill
Global Cause Consultancy
Jack Gordon & Kate Lacy
Richard Gordon
Hugh & Sarah Grootenhuis
Thea Guest
Lesley Hill & Russ Shaw
Madeleine Hodgkin
Bea Hollond
Caroline Howlett
Ann & Ravi Joseph
Davina & Malcolm Judelson
Kristen Kennish
Nicola Kerr
Sue Knox
Isabella Macpherson
Penny Marland
Liz & Luke Mayhew
Michael McCoy
Fiona McDougall
Judith Mellor
Caro Millington
Ann Montier
Georgia Oetker
Mark & Anne Paterson
Lauren Prakke
Barbara Prideaux
Emily Reeve
Renske & Marion
Sarah Richards
John Seal and Karen Scofield
Jon & NoraLee Sedmak
John & Tita Shakeshaft
Diane Sheridan
Saleem & Alexandra Siddiqi
Melanie Slimmon
Brian Smith
Nick Starr
Ed Vaizey
Marina Vaizey
Francois & Arrelle von Hurter
Trish Wadley
Amanda Waggott
Sir Robert & Lady Wilson
Peter Wilson-Smith & Kat Callo
Alison Winter
Andrew & Carey Wright

If you are interested in finding out how to be involved, please visit the 'Support Us' section of bushtheatre.co.uk, email development@bushtheatre.co.uk or call 020 8743 3584.

CORPORATE MEMBERS

LEADING LIGHT
Winston Capital Management

LIGHTBULB
The Agency (London) Ltd

SPONSORS & SUPPORTERS
Drama Centre London
Kudos Film & TV
MAC Cosmetics
Markson Pianos
Finlay Brewer
The Groucho Club
The Law Society
Ideas Tap
Waitrose Community Matters
West 12 Shopping & Leisure Centre

TRUSTS & FOUNDATIONS
The Andrew Lloyd Webber Foundation
The Austin and Hope Pilkington Trust
BBC Performing Arts Fund
The City Bridge Trust
Coutts Charitable Trust
The Daisy Trust
The D'Oyly Carte Charitable Trust
EC&O Venues Charitable Trust
The Equity Charitable Trust
Fidelio Charitable Trust
Foundation for Sport and the Arts
Garfield Weston Foundation
Garrick Charitable Trust
The Gatsby Charitable Foundation
The Goldsmiths' Company
Hammersmith United Charities
The Harold Hyam Wingate Foundation
The Idlewild Trust
Japan Foundation
Jerwood Charitable Foundation
John Lyon's Charity
The J Paul Getty Jnr Charitable Trust
The John Thaw Foundation
The Laurie & Gillian Marsh Charitable Trust
The Leverhulme Trust
The Martin Bowley Charitable Trust
Royal Victoria Hall Foundation
Sir Siegmund Warburg's Voluntary Settlement
Sita Trust
The Theatres Trust
The Thistle Trust
The Williams Charitable Trust
The Worshipful Company of Grocers

PUBLIC FUNDING

The Age of Loneliness is Killing Us

by George Monbiot

The age we are entering, in which we exist apart, is unlike any that has gone before. This is the Age of Loneliness. We were social creatures from the start, mammalian bees, who depended entirely on each other. We are shaped, to a greater extent than almost any other species, by contact with others. But now, social isolation is as potent a cause of early death as smoking 15 cigarettes a day; loneliness, research suggests, is twice as deadly as obesity. Dementia, high blood pressure, alcoholism and accidents – all these, like depression, paranoia, anxiety and suicide, become more prevalent when connections are cut. We cannot cope alone. Yet what counts now is to win. The rest is collateral damage.

British children no longer aspire to be train drivers or nurses – more than a fifth say they 'just want to be rich': wealth and fame are the sole ambitions of 40% of those surveyed. A government study in June revealed that Britain is the loneliness capital of Europe. Who can be surprised, when everywhere we are urged to fight like stray dogs over a dustbin?

Our most cutting insult is 'loser'. We no longer talk about people. Now we call them individuals. Competition drives growth, but growth no longer makes us wealthier. Figures published this week show that, while the income of company directors has risen by more than a fifth, wages for the workforce as a whole have fallen in real terms over the past year. The bosses earn – sorry, I mean take – 120 times more than the average full-time worker. (In 2000, it was 47 times.)

Yet, a survey by Boston College of people with an average net worth of $78m found that they too were assailed by anxiety, dissatisfaction and loneliness. Many of them reported feeling financially insecure: to reach safe ground, they believed, they would need, on average, about 25% more money.

And for this, we have ripped the natural world apart, degraded our conditions of life, surrendered our freedoms and prospects of contentment to a compulsive, atomising, joyless hedonism, in which, having consumed all else, we start to prey upon ourselves. For this, we have destroyed the essence of humanity: our connectedness.

This is an extract of an article originally published by the *Guardian* in October 2014. Reproduced by kind permission of the author.

www.guardian.co.uk
www.monbiot.com

FUCK THE POLAR BEARS

Tanya Ronder

Acknowledgements

My thanks to Madani Younis and his team at the Bush for their priceless parenting of a young idea – they are truly a writer's theatre.

Grateful thanks to those who stoked the fire along the way – Sophie Wu, Monica Dolan, Mark Lockyer, Kobna Holdbrook-Smith, Karen Cogan, Michael Shaeffer, Richard Hawley, Lyndsey Marshal, Katie West, Danny Webb, Isabella Laughland, Jessica Sian, Chook Sibtain and Roger Michell.

And for reading – Darragh, Jules, Ruth, Rose, Louis, Deborah, Rufus, Emma Jane and Nick Hern.

To crucial and open conversations regarding the facts – Juliet Davenport, Lavan Rubasingam and Alastair Harper, thank you; thanks also to Tipping Point, and for the inspiration of writers Naomi Klein, George Monbiot and Elizabeth Kolbert.

And my deep thanks to Caroline Byrne and her team, who engaged with such forensic precision and huge open hearts with everything that the piece asks.

T.R.

Most of us can read the writing on the wall;
we just assume it's addressed to someone else.

Ivern Ball

To the shared art of keepy-uppy

Characters

GORDON, *Communications Director of a big energy company*
SERENA, *his wife*
BLUNDHILDE, *their au pair*
RACHEL, *their young daughter*
CLARENCE, *Gordon's brother*

This text went to press before the end of rehearsals and so may differ slightly from the play as performed.

ACT ONE

Scene One

Friday evening

A smooth car pulls up on gravel. The central hallway/open living area of an ostentatious house in North London. Large enough to house a backless divan/daybed, all the action takes place in this space. We hear the front door close, the inner door open, a slight curse, then GORDON *arrives with a door handle in his hand. He is laden – doorknob, briefcase, pizzas, off-licence bag.* SERENA *calls.*

SERENA (*off*). Is that you?

GORDON (*calls back*). Hello, lollipop.

SERENA (*off*). Hi, I'm just…

GORDON. Don't worry. Rache?

(*Calls.*) Rachel?

SERENA (*off*). She's at Helen's.

    SERENA *dashes in with a girl's bag. These two are down-to-earth people come to money late, not posh at all.* SERENA, *younger than* GORDON, *has a strong Irish or regional accent,* GORDON *is from London or the regions. Their conversation is fast and pinched.*

You're late.

He puts down his stuff to help.

GORDON. What can I do?

SERENA. Did that just – ?

GORDON. Clarence can –

SERENA. Yep.

    Beat.

You got my text?

GORDON. What did he say?

SERENA. That we're being gazumped, in his agent way…

GORDON. Don't panic, Serena…

SERENA. It's reasonable panic, Gordon, I don't know why you're not.

GORDON. It's my job not to.

SERENA. This is home, Gord, not work, your serenity's all wrong here.

GORDON. Can't help it, when stress comes up I just say no.

SERENA. Whereas I actually make huge efforts to feel uptight all the time.

Beat.

Did you get it?

GORDON. I've come straight from a meet.

SERENA. Via Pizza Dome…

GORDON. With a pretty spectacular outcome.

SERENA. But no bonus.

GORDON. I didn't want to ask for what is essentially a Christmas present in September.

They start talking over each other.

SERENA. Nearly October –

GORDON. You know what I'm saying –

SERENA. Why did you say you were going to, then?

GORDON. Because –

SERENA. You went this morning saying you would ask.

GORDON. Were there no alternative. A bonus is finite.

SERENA. I know it's fucking finite – yes I know I swore, I'll put a pound in the box –

GORDON. I'm getting you your house, my love –

SERENA. What if we get another offer, lose that buyer too, and it's not my fucking house. (*Swear box.*) I know.

GORDON. Serena, listen, I know it's not in the bank –

SERENA. Which is where it needs to be –

GORDON. But, but it will be by Monday. Trust me, we'll come in, bang, with anything they need, blow everything else out the water.

SERENA. How?

GORDON. I'm in a completely different scenario than I was twelve hours ago.

SERENA. Did you molest someone, you been arrested?

He appreciates her humour.

GORDON. What time are you leaving?

SERENA *catches sight of the time.*

SERENA. Oh God, where's Blundhilde... (*Calls off.*) Blundhilde?

BLUNDHILDE *replies from upstairs.*

BLUNDHILDE (*off*). Coming!

GORDON. We're safe, my sweetheart, trust me.

SERENA. Apart from having to find several million over the weekend.

GORDON. High streets are not the only option.

SERENA *changes her mind, calls back up to* BLUNDHILDE.

SERENA. In fact, not yet, don't come down yet, five minutes, Blundhilde, okay? Blundhilde? Come down in five.

BLUNDHILDE (*off*). Okay, Serena!

SERENA (*to* GORDON). Hold there just one sec.

SERENA *runs to the utility room, the sound of a tumble dryer opening.*

(*Off.*) Shit.

The tumble dryer closes, starts up again. GORDON *shouts through to her.*

GORDON. What time are you back?

SERENA (*off*). Clarence is here later.

SERENA *comes back in.*

What's the crux?

GORDON. Salary increase.

Beat.

Can we have coffee tomorrow?

SERENA. I'm not here tomorrow.

GORDON. Course.

SERENA. We could at midnight or dawn.

She dashes into an adjacent room.

A walk in the park is like some dream from the past.

She emerges with a brush.

I'm so crap, I always forget her hairbrush.

GORDON. D'you want some pizza before you go?

SERENA. Maybe, it's just a bit…

She makes a face.

But, it's Friday.

GORDON. Is that why you only have *me* on Fridays? Bit –

He returns the face.

SERENA. You can talk, Mr Distracted…

GORDON. I'm never not up for nookie.

SERENA. Huh.

GORDON. With my beautiful wife.

He approaches her.

SERENA. Not now, Gord, everyone's… everything's…

GORDON *takes the pizzas and crosses to the kitchen.*

I've just sorted in there.

He turns back.

GORDON. It's why I got pizza instead of Chinese or…

SERENA. What flavour?

GORDON. Sloppy Giuseppe.

SERENA. How many?

GORDON. Six.

SERENA. Six?

GORDON. Plus…

He reveals the champagne, gets two flutes.

SERENA. What's the increase?

He pops the cork.

GORDON. Substantial. I have to go against Wiggie but that's not a problem, I can do that, I can do anything.

His confidence deflates SERENA. *The upstairs toilet flushes.* GORDON *pours champagne.*

SERENA. I'm not drinking.

GORDON. Why not?

SERENA. Driving.

GORDON. Course you are.

SERENA looks at her watch.

What do we have to do?

SERENA. 'We'.

She says this almost to herself.

GORDON. Do you want me to get her?

SERENA. It's fine, Blundhilde can go, they just eat so early in that house, as if I needed that detail. Do you know what Helen's mum's mother's name is?

GORDON. No.

SERENA. Or that she has a colostomy bag?

GORDON. I didn't, no. I thought you liked Helen's mum.

SERENA. I do, but I don't need to know where her mother hangs her...

SERENA puts toothbrushes in Ziploc plastic bags, etc.

GORDON. You're plugged into the world, my love, which is a good thing.

SERENA. I've got the surface stuff covered, which was the height of my ambition...

GORDON. That's why you're doing your Body Balance, babe.

Eating pizza.

It's like a working dinner.

SERENA. Fuck off, Gordon.

GORDON. I'm trying really hard here, Serena...

SERENA. Your work is awesome and complicated, so how is being home like work?

GORDON swallows his feelings, tries to calm her.

GORDON. I know it's a pressured time. Moving house is –

SERENA. More stressful than divorce. I need the dryer to finish.

He doesn't understand, she whispers fiercely.

Before Blundhilde comes down.

Beat.

Sorry for telling you to fuck off. I know. (*Swear box.*)

GORDON. Unusual response to being guaranteed the house of your dreams.

SERENA. Don't talk guarantees. And it's not for me we're doing these things, it's for us, isn't it, you need it more than any of us.

GORDON. I want you to be happy.

SERENA. Do you know how lonely that makes me feel, you buying a house to cheer up miseryguts me.

GORDON. I'm not saying you're miserable, I just want us to enjoy our lives.

SERENA. And so we should, lucky beggars, with our Sloppy Giuseppe and our champagne.

BLUNDHILDE *comes downstairs*.

GORDON. Evening, Blundhilde.

BLUNDHILDE. Hi.

GORDON. Would you like some pizza?

SERENA. Rache might want a slither in the car, actually, would you mind doing that, Blundhilde? There's new foil in the kitchen.

BLUNDHILDE. Is that the tumble dryer?

SERENA. It's just a really quick blast...

BLUNDHILDE. It was beautiful today –

SERENA. And there's miles of line out there, I know.

BLUNDHILDE. You should have said, I would have hung it out for you.

SERENA. But I opted for the high-energy option, okay, is that okay?

Beat.

It's her skull-and-crossbone pyjamas, I forgot to wash them earlier, she's not seen her godmother since she gave them to her last Christmas.

BLUNDHILDE. Is everything all right, Serena?

SERENA. Fine, why?

BLUNDHILDE. Are you annoyed about something?

SERENA. Just knackered, Blundhilde. Why don't you pop and get Rache, then we can head off.

BLUNDHILDE. Of course.

BLUNDHILDE gets out a reusable sandwich-wrap to put the pizza in.

Did you find Phoebe?

SERENA. No, that's the other thing…

GORDON. Phoebe?

SERENA. Can't find her.

GORDON. What do you mean you can't find her?

SERENA. She's disappeared.

Beat.

BLUNDHILDE breaks the moment to quietly ask.

BLUNDHILDE. Should I take some for you too, Serena?

SERENA. No, I'm fine. Is that your *petite* or your *grande* Snack-Taxi?

BLUNDHILDE. It's the big one.

She packs the pizza away.

Okay, see you.

GORDON makes an effort to be friendly to make up for SERENA.

GORDON. See you soon, Blundhilde.

BLUNDHILDE leaves.

SERENA (*speaks under her breath*). I'm such a bitch.

GORDON. You're not a bitch.

The front door slams.

SERENA. She winds me up.

GORDON. She's great with Rache…

SERENA. I know, or I'd have sacked her by now!

Half beat.

They're so damn rare, those houses, every day more people are asking, it's still on all the websites, they won't take it off.

GORDON. That's why we're going all out.

SERENA. For me.

GORDON. For you, for me and for our beloved...

Beat. He can't mention RACHEL *in this sentence.*

SERENA. Little girl. Do you know what a bridging loan costs?

GORDON. No more than we save from having Blundhilde instead of a nanny.

SERENA. A French woman from class is paying twenty-seven thousand a month, I'm not joking, show me a nanny who charges that.

GORDON. Thirty grand a month, Serena, will soon be an irrelevance to us.

Beat.

SERENA. You're going to have to work even harder, come home even less.

GORDON. It's what we want, isn't it?

They move towards one another. SERENA *sees his jacket.*

SERENA. What's that?

He hides the stain.

GORDON. I thought I'd got it off.

SERENA. Who threw eggs at you?

GORDON. Some anti-fracking munter.

SERENA. Again? Where?

GORDON. Westminster.

SERENA. Egg's a monster to clean because it's protein.

GORDON. I know.

SERENA. It clings.

GORDON. Don't mention it to Rache.

SERENA. Blundhilde told me that when you get clothes home from the cleaners the chemicals linger in the house and penetrate your lungs.

GORDON. How should we get it off?

SERENA. I'll take it to the cleaners on Monday. Did I leave a blue plastic bag in your car with Rachel's Banana Guard in and a bottle of flaxseed oil?

GORDON. I love you, lollipop.

SERENA. Why? D'you expect no more of me than this?

GORDON. Than what?

SERENA. This piece-of-shit kind of life.

He exhales, drinks.

I can't have sex now, Gordon, please don't look disappointed.

Beat.

GORDON. Looking forward to your training?

SERENA. It couldn't have fallen on a worse weekend, plus they'll all be younger and fitter than me.

GORDON. They don't come much fitter than you.

SERENA. You live in cuckoo land.

She goes off, the sound of the tumble dryer opening and slamming.

(*Off.*) They take for fucking ever, these dryers.

(*Shouts through to* GORDON.) Yes, the box, for God's sakes don't tell Rache.

She comes through.

Are you talking CEO, Gord?

Beat.

Honestly?

GORDON. Honestly.

SERENA. What's the salary?

GORDON. Two point four million.

SERENA. Fuck.

GORDON. That's what Wiggie earns.

SERENA. Wow, Gordon.

Beat.

I could teach Body Balance in the attic, if I qualify.

GORDON. Course you'll qualify.

SERENA. Did you know that the Lemon Tree rents out its conservatory?

GORDON. I didn't, no.

SERENA. I'm jumping the gun but maybe I could start a Balance class there as well. Without the drive to school I get three hours of my day back!

GORDON *enjoys* SERENA*'s pleasure.*

We could fly Mum and Bridget and the kids over for the house-warming, open the back all up. We might have to have those blasty heaters that look like fires, the kids would love that, unless Blundhilde's still with us, in which case we'd have to light a proper fire like cavemen. The first thing to do is secure the railings down the bottom so there's no possibility of anyone falling in…

GORDON. I could give the kids boat rides on the river.

SERENA. Oh, Gord, it's such a haven, easy for work and ten minutes from the best girls' prep in London, what more can parents do?

GORDON*'s champagne glass smashes.*

Shit!

GORDON. Shit.

SERENA. How did that happen?

GORDON. I've no idea.

SERENA. That's freaky.

GORDON. I didn't squeeze it or anything… it's like a bomb, it's everywhere.

SERENA. A self-combusting glass. Are you okay?

GORDON. I'm fine.

> GORDON *starts to clear it up.*

Can you pass that newspaper? We should throw the rest of this away.

SERENA. Fortunately there are five other unopened ones…

> *He gathers the broken glass and open pizza box.*

I'll get the dustbuster.

> *She opens a new box.*

That actually smells really good.

> *She eats some pizza.*

Our nicest glasses, those, it must have had a crack…

GORDON. Yeah.

> SERENA *stops eating.*

SERENA. Uh.

GORDON. What?

SERENA. Something just crunched.

GORDON. Really?

SERENA. Mmm, that felt peculiar.

GORDON. Did you swallow?

SERENA. Mmm.

GORDON. It's fine, I'm sure it's fine, but you should eat something to bulk it out so it can't cut anything on the way down –

SERENA. Like my jugular?

GORDON. Bread, maybe, or peanut butter, something with some stick to it…

He goes to look for some.

A piece must have snuck in the side of the box.

Half beat.

SERENA. Do you only not want me to die because you'd worry you'd killed me?

GORDON. What?

SERENA. I'm a nightmare, aren't I? At least your first marriage was calm.

GORDON. Serena…

SERENA. Sometimes I think you wish you'd never married me.

GORDON. You're the one who's angry.

SERENA. The one who mouths off, maybe.

GORDON. Do you wish you'd never married me?

SERENA. I'm not the one who feeds you glass.

GORDON. I don't feed you glass!

They hear the key in the lock.

SERENA. Ssh, they'll know we're fighting.

GORDON. We're not. Drink this.

He hands her a glass of water.

SERENA. From the tap?

GORDON. We're out of bottled.

SERENA. There's more in the garage…

She sips.

Tastes of chlorine.

GORDON. Means it's clean.

The door slams, GORDON *shouts cheerfully through to the hallway.*

Hi, gorgeous, how's my girl?

We hear BLUNDHILDE *and* RACHEL *in the vestibule.*

BLUNDHILDE (*off*). You going to hang your coat up?

SERENA. Shit.

SERENA rushes off. GORDON *calls after her.*

GORDON. What? You found Phoebe? Serena, what is it?

BLUNDHILDE (*off*) Whoops, the hook's coming loose…

We hear the tumble dryer opening. SERENA *curses.*

SERENA (*off*). I should have hung the bloody things outside!

Blackout.

End of Scene.

Scene Two

Friday night

Later the same evening, GORDON, *alone, speaks privately to someone we can't see.*

GORDON. I know you're somewhere, 'cause I know what you're up to. I am on to you, as you are on to me.

The doorbell rings.

And you know what, Phoebe, you're right to be hiding.

GORDON *answers the door.*

CLARENCE. Yo, bro.

GORDON. What's up?

CLARENCE. I'm good, very good. You?

GORDON. Heroic, we're smashing it. Is that the old van?

CLARENCE. Yeah…

GORDON. Still going?

CLARENCE. Just about.

They come through. CLARENCE *carries a painting kit, a box of eggs and a small polar bear with a card.*

It's very quiet, where is everyone?

GORDON. We wanted Rache out the way.

CLARENCE. Oh.

GORDON. She's gone to her godmother's.

CLARENCE. 'Cause of paint fumes?

GORDON. You got the fancy stuff, didn't you?

CLARENCE. I did.

GORDON. Serena was very particular…

CLARENCE. I got it.

GORDON. So no, not fumes, just while we get the house spick and span.

Beat.

CLARENCE. How are they both?

GORDON. Legends, the pair of them. You'll see Serena later, she's back to do this training thing.

CLARENCE. What's she training in?

GORDON. Kind of yoga but not quite.

CLARENCE. Oh right, great.

CLARENCE *hands* GORDON *the eggs.*

Home grown by my other half.

GORDON. We won't get hangovers off those.

Beat.

CLARENCE. One of the upsides of living lightly.

GORDON. Who's the other half?

CLARENCE. Oh, you know, my girlfriend. Well, woman-friend.

GORDON. What, no sex?

CLARENCE. No, not no sex, I just meant, not a girl, as such…

GORDON. Name?

CLARENCE. Irene.

GORDON. Is Irene married?

CLARENCE. No.

GORDON. Is she a looker, is she?

CLARENCE. Not officially a looker, Gordon, no.

GORDON's phone rings, he jumps for it.

GORDON. 'Scuse me, I'm expecting a call.

He snatches up the phone, it's charging so he has to stoop to speak.

Hello, hello, mate?

There's no one there. He looks at phone.

Don't know what that was.

The phone rings again. He looks, it's a different number.

Oh, okay. Yup?

BLUNDHILDE (*on phone*). Gordon, it's Blundhilde…

GORDON. Yup, hi, I'm still looking, can't find her anywhere.

He puts it on speaker so he can stand up. From the car, through the phone, RACHEL *wails.*

RACHEL (*on phone*). Phoebe?

BLUNDHILDE (*on phone*). She just wants to say goodnight…

GORDON. Yeah, course she does, I know she does.

BLUNDHILDE (*on phone*). Okay, thanks, Gordon. Give us a ring if she turns up.

In the background RACHEL *wails again.*

RACHEL (*on phone*). Find Phoebe!

GORDON. I'm doing my best, my angel!

He closes his phone.

You remember Phoebe?

CLARENCE. Rachel's polar bear?

GORDON. She's lost.

CLARENCE. Oh, no. I brought her a baby one.

GORDON. I saw.

CLARENCE. Son of Phoebe.

Half beat.

But, obviously, if she's lost Phoebe…

Beat.

Does she still think she's real?

GORDON. Yeah.

CLARENCE. Everyone was writing notes last time I was here, from Phoebe. *'Mmm, chocolate…!'*, then when Rachel turned her back you'd eat it…

He does the voice of young RACHEL.

'Phoebe, you're such a greedy guts!'

GORDON. I'm impressed you remember.

Half beat.

CLARENCE. I'm sorry to miss her.

GORDON. You might see her, depends if you're a painter or a tosher.

CLARENCE. Did you call me a tosser?

GORDON. Tosher, you tosser. Do you throw the paint on or do you do a proper job?

CLARENCE. Why would I not do it properly? It's my trade, it's your house.

GORDON. It's for selling, not to live in.

CLARENCE. But somebody'll live here.

GORDON. They'll repaint. Have we talked money?

CLARENCE. Don't worry about it.

GORDON. Family-and-friends rate for your old bro?

CLARENCE. It's a gift, Gordon, a thank-you for your help.

GORDON. Don't turn all Jesus on me, Clarence.

CLARENCE. It's not exactly Messianic to say thank you.

GORDON. Right then, gift accepted. To be honest it'll help
with cash flow.

CLARENCE. Yeah?

GORDON. Even us rich bastards have our moments. But it
won't last long.

He takes a step backwards and trips over the little bear.

Aagh!

CLARENCE. Is he all right?

GORDON. What about me? It's not fucking funny.

CLARENCE. D'you remember you always got clumsy when
you were in trouble?

GORDON. No.

CLARENCE. When you had all those stolen razors under your
bed and kept dropping your fork at dinner.

GORDON. What's wrong with you?

CLARENCE. Or when you two-timed Theresa Manning and
couldn't stop bashing in to lamp posts!

GORDON. Stop talking bollocks, and which of us is the two-
timer of the family?

Beat.

CLARENCE. Janey sends her love by the way.

GORDON. '*Janey*' now, is it?

CLARENCE. Jane.

GORDON. She your best friend?

CLARENCE. No, she's my ex-sister-in-law… She's only along the coast.

GORDON. How is she, still in her dead-end job?

CLARENCE. She runs the charity now, spends all her weekends taking city kids up on the Downs, she loves it.

GORDON. Well, what else are you going to do with your weekends with no kids of your own.

Beat.

CLARENCE. So what's the house like?

GORDON. What d'you mean?

CLARENCE. Your new one.

GORDON. Stunning.

CLARENCE. Yeah?

GORDON. Historic and very peaceful. Do you know Hampton?

CLARENCE. No.

GORDON. There's a row on the river, it's the last house.

CLARENCE. Great. You were always ambitious for that stuff, weren't you.

GORDON. What stuff?

CLARENCE. Big houses and that.

GORDON. It's an exceptional place.

CLARENCE. I'm sure.

GORDON. Show me someone who doesn't dream of having that. Who wouldn't, if they had the money, live on the best bit of river in the best city in the world in a house to die for with its own private jetty?

CLARENCE. Dad would be proud.

GORDON. When are you going to make Mum proud?

CLARENCE. I think she is proud. Talking of which, I'm hoping we might have five minutes while I'm here, the two of us, there are some things I'd like to say.

GORDON. You've said thanks.

CLARENCE. I know.

GORDON. You've said it.

CLARENCE. It would mean a lot.

GORDON *doesn't want to hear.*

GORDON. Seen Mum recently?

CLARENCE. I see her every week.

GORDON. Since when? Man, can you smell that? I keep getting a whiff of drains.

CLARENCE. You been letting off?

GORDON. Grow up, Clarence. You know how things always come –

CLARENCE. In threes.

GORDON. I've had a day of it. So, yeah, it's, uh, mainly the hallway upstairs and the other bits we talked about.

Half beat.

CLARENCE. I'll start prepping.

GORDON. And. If you come across Phoebe…

CLARENCE. Course.

GORDON*'s phone dings, he checks it.*

GORDON. What do you mean nineteen per cent, you've been charging all night, I watched you turn green! (*To* CLARENCE.) Did you see a green light?

CLARENCE. I didn't notice.

GORDON. That was definitely –

CLARENCE. Maybe it's the connector.

GORDON. It's a new charger, that.

He reads his text.

Oh fuck, he's on holiday.

CLARENCE. Who?

GORDON. Never mind. Mr Cash Flow.

CLARENCE's phone dings. He checks his message and laughs.

What's funny?

CLARENCE. Irene's just sent a picture of her granddaughter.

GORDON. Granddaughter?

CLARENCE. She's only eight months.

GORDON. So Irene's a blue rinse.

CLARENCE. She has a little grey pixie cut, actually, very cute.

GORDON. Bully for you, with your Help-the-Aged girlfriend and your do-gooding attitude.

He trips up again.

Fuck!

CLARENCE. You've grown two left feet, Gord, chill out.

GORDON. Don't patronise me, you little bastard.

CLARENCE. Come on, I'm your brother, I've not seen you in two years, I'm just trying to –

GORDON. Just paint my walls and shut the fuck up.

Beat.

End of Act.

ACT TWO

Scene One

Saturday morning

Dust sheets are down, CLARENCE *prepares Polyfilla.*
SERENA *hurries on.*

SERENA. Do you have everything you need?

CLARENCE. I think so, thanks.

She checks the paint.

SERENA. That's great you found the 'bone'. I'm not sure our
bones are actually that colour. I hope it works with the carpet
up there. I know it's pricier but you can't sell a house these
days without it, everyone's become so damn chic. Probably
the reason our buyer pulled out, 'cause we didn't have it on
the walls. Just add the cost to your bill, will you, Clarence?

CLARENCE. Uh, actually…

CLARENCE *tries to say there will be no bill but* SERENA
whizzes into the kitchen not noticing.

SERENA (*off*). The open house is Monday at five… needs
must, you know, got to push for your dreams. Would you like
a cup of tea, Clarence?

CLARENCE. No thanks, Serena, I'm fine.

GORDON *walks through in a towel.*

SERENA. In the new place I want one of those things that does
boiling water on tap.

CLARENCE. Oh right?

SERENA. How lovely will that be, like on the Starship
Enterprise or something.

CLARENCE. I enjoy waiting for the kettle to boil, it's a tiny
pause in the day.

SERENA. Dead time, drives me crazy.

CLARENCE. I don't think I'd feel I'd actually made a cup of tea with one of those things.

SERENA. Really?

CLARENCE. If you don't knead the bread, did you make the loaf, if you don't stir the gloop, have you baked the cake?

SERENA. If you don't pilot the plane, have you landed? Tea is tea is tea, surely.

CLARENCE. I bet they guzzle energy.

SERENA. Don't start. No more than boiling kettles, apparently.

CLARENCE. Says who?

SERENA. The manufacturers. It doesn't cost any more anyway, beyond the initial outlay obviously, but, you know, economy, ecology, it all merges into one. Did Gordon disturb you last night? I got back in the early hours and he was breathing like a train in a tunnel –

She does a half-voiced impression.

Heurgh, heurgh, heurgh… Did you hear the debacle of us losing Rachel's bear?

CLARENCE. Yeah, poor little Rache.

SERENA. I slept with her for hours she was so upset and I've got this training today, got to bed stupidly late of course.

She catches sight of the time.

Oh god, I'm sorry, Clarence, I have to go over something on the computer…

CLARENCE. Am I in your way?

SERENA. No, you're fine, I'll just…

She goes to put it on, a bit embarrassed.

Crap, I just turned it off, Macs do my head in. Are you Apple?

CLARENCE. No.

SERENA. It took me twenty-seven sessions to get on top of my MacBook.

CLARENCE. Yeah?

SERENA. Yeah. Twenty-seven sessions in Covent Garden.
Anyway, they told me to always leave it on standby, but then
everyone who's sensitive about these things or, basically,
Blundhilde, our au pair, says turn everything off when you're
not using them. She's got a thing about the blinking eyes,
you know, I mean she has a point but she even says you
should switch sockets off at walls when you're not actually
using your charger or whatever, but she's from Iceland and
frankly, you know, what's life about? And honestly I still
don't know if it's bad to keep things on standby because we
get infra rays or whatever damaging our brains or if it wastes
electricity, or is it the money? If it is money it doesn't affect
us in this house so much because we get a discount on our
energy bills, obviously, because of Gordon, plus the more
energy people use, the more he gets paid so, that's a bit
confusing. Or is it, you know, because it adds to the ozone
layer. That suddenly makes me feel really old because
nobody even talks about the ozone any more, I don't even
know where that came from... what happened to the ozone?
Anyway, you know what I mean, the we're-all-going-to-die,
bit of strong wind and whoops-the-world's-ending thing.

CLARENCE. Emissions and stuff.

SERENA. Exactly, hothouse, greenhouse, poor Gordon can't
move for the jargon. Anyway, didn't mean to start a doom-
and-gloom chat, sorry I'm talking too much, I always do
when I'm nervous, feel sick about today.

The screen springs to life. The footage is of SERENA
teaching. The sound is down.

Don't look. It sounds an awful hotchpotch, but I actually
really love it, it's a mixture of t'ai chi, yoga and Pilates. But
they make you do this awful video of yourself teaching
which is obviously...

*She turns it up slightly, counts the beats as she synchs with
her screen-self doing a customised t'ai-chi move to a rousing
pop anthem.*

One, two, three, four, five, six, seven, eight, one, two, three,
four, five, six, seven, eight... (*Etc.*)

CLARENCE. That looks great.

SERENA. I said don't! Oh, I nearly forgot, can you take the bolt off the playroom door? I don't want people thinking we're monsters, maybe that's why the buyers pulled out!

CLARENCE. I'm sure not.

SERENA. The naughty step never worked for Rache, she just got off, but two minutes in there was brilliant, honestly.

CLARENCE. Is she quite naughty now?

SERENA. You two were close, weren't you? She's just a bit bolshie, we've not used it for ages. Oh, and also, did Gordon show you the doorknob he managed to pull off yesterday?

GORDON *comes back from the utility room.*

Gordon?

GORDON. Yeah?

SERENA. Will you show Clarence the door handle and also, promise you'll call the plumber if you can't fix the drain?

GORDON. Yeah.

SERENA. Why are you showering before clearing drains?

GORDON. I'm not.

She looks at him in his towel.

Hot water's not working.

SERENA. You're joking.

GORDON. Pressure was down, I'm trying again.

SERENA. Are you okay?

GORDON. Yes, why?

She does an impression of his train breathing.

SERENA. Heurgh, heurgh, heurgh...

GORDON *explains to* CLARENCE.

GORDON. I was snoring.

CLARENCE. She said.

SERENA. More like roaring.

SERENA *addresses* GORDON.

Can I ask you a quick question?

GORDON. Yeah.

She turns and shows him her bum.

Gorgeous, sexy, like a teacher… anything else?

SERENA. Believe what you say.

GORDON. It's you who doesn't believe it.

SERENA *has her back to* CLARENCE.

CLARENCE. I know it's not a brother-in-law's place, but.

He holds up two enthusiastic thumbs.

SERENA. Thanks, Clarence. Where are you living these days?

CLARENCE. Shoreham-by-Sea.

BLUNDHILDE *comes gingerly in with a light bulb – the glass separated from the metal.*

BLUNDHILDE. The light just blew on the landing.

SERENA. What!

BLUNDHILDE (*dryly*). Sorry.

CLARENCE. The three-for-a-pound ones always do that.

GORDON. There are more in the cupboard, not from Poundland.

BLUNDHILDE. Eco ones?

SERENA. No.

BLUNDHILDE *goes to the kitchen.*

(*To* GORDON.) About the drains, are you emptying the coffee pot down the sink again?

BLUNDHILDE *pipes up from the kitchen.*

BLUNDHILDE. Coffee grains go in the green bin.

SERENA. Precisely, Gordon.

CLARENCE. Irene puts hers on the garden, or down the toilet if it's parky…

GORDON. It'll be a plastic bag or somebody's takeaway.

CLARENCE. I still can't smell the drains.

SERENA. Nor me, actually.

SERENA *speaks to* CLARENCE.

Last time the drains blocked, three men in long boots came to clear them, solid grease clumped with coffee and I won't begin to say what else, and the pipes go all the way under the house, you know. D'you know what had caused the blockage?

CLARENCE. No.

SERENA. Rats, got in through a hole in the path. Do you have a wet room at home?

CLARENCE. No.

SERENA. We have here and I watched one of those plumbers lift the cover and clean out the bit that's like the plughole? Disgusting, just from humans washing. Pale slimy sludge embedded with hair. It needs cleaning once a fortnight, apparently, I can't ask Blundhilde or the cleaner to do that, can I? And of course, Gordon's not touched it once. I'd better go, I'm going to be late.

GORDON. Go, babe.

SERENA. First day and all, wish me luck!

CLARENCE. Bye, Serena, good luck.

She leaves. BLUNDHILDE *comes out with a new bulb.*

GORDON. If you hear me cursing, put the kettle on.

BLUNDHILDE. You could have a cold shower, that's what they do in –

He cuts her off.

GORDON. Mad-land.

He goes back upstairs.

BLUNDHILDE. Hi.

CLARENCE. Hi.

BLUNDHILDE. I'm Blundhilde, the au pair.

CLARENCE. I'm Clarence.

BLUNDHILDE. Gordon's brother?

CLARENCE. Yup.

BLUNDHILDE. You've not seen a polar bear, have you?

CLARENCE. Phoebe?

BLUNDHILDE. I have to find her and take her on the train to Cobham. I'm meant to be seeing a film with a friend, it's my day off.

CLARENCE. Sure you've not hidden her, in that case.

BLUNDHILDE *is a bit serious*.

BLUNDHILDE. I wouldn't do that. Did you see her last night?

CLARENCE. No.

He's trying to get on with his work.

BLUNDHILDE. Have you seen her since the eyes?

CLARENCE *looks baffled*.

She got so dirty from Rachel dragging her round everywhere that we washed her in the bath then hung her out to dry, but Rachel wanted her that night in bed so Serena put her in the tumble dryer but the plastic on the eyes melted. Now she looks like she's always looking at you, wherever you are in the room. While she was hanging on the line the neighbours, Geoff and Dilys, saw her and thought she was a dog. Their dog had just died so they didn't speak to Serena for a long time, Dilys is quite paranoid. I'd better call Rachel.

CLARENCE. Go to your film instead?

BLUNDHILDE. I have to say goodbye to someone, she's leaving tomorrow.

CLARENCE. Oh right, a friend?

BLUNDHILDE. More than a friend.

CLARENCE. Oh.

BLUNDHILDE. A lover.

CLARENCE. Oh.

BLUNDHILDE. I'd not been with a girl before Pepper Anne.

CLARENCE. Okay.

BLUNDHILDE. Just boys, mostly Australians. Anyway, she's moving back to Holland to volunteer.

CLARENCE. Good for her, who's she working for?

BLUNDHILDE. The Zwaar Weer Cooperative.

CLARENCE. Zwaar Weer?

BLUNDHILDE. Heavy Weather.

CLARENCE. Nice that you're seeing a last film together.

BLUNDHILDE. We're not, I'm seeing the film with another friend, but it starts at twelve forty-five and Pepper Anne's last shift finishes at three and it's only round the corner because she works in Pret in Covent Garden and the film is at the Prince Charles Cinema. She used to work in Food for Thought but it's closed down.

CLARENCE. Is that that salad place?

BLUNDHILDE. Yeah. I'm a vegetarian. Five days a week.

CLARENCE. Oh.

BLUNDHILDE. The fuel you use to drive twenty miles in a Mini?

CLARENCE. Yeah.

BLUNDHILDE. Is what it takes to produce a steak.

CLARENCE. Really?

BLUNDHILDE. Yeah. Or a burger.

CLARENCE. Twenty miles.

BLUNDHILDE. Because the pigs and cows eat so much.

The toilet flushes upstairs.

So, like, growing crops for them uses all this water.

GORDON *comes bounding down the stairs.*

GORDON. Time to face my drains.

CLARENCE. Did you get your shower?

GORDON. Yep, though somebody's moved my weekend trousers, oh and, Blundhilde, was it you who turned off the fridge freezer?

BLUNDHILDE. No.

GORDON. I had a kilo of top-notch Spanish ham in there which is now too soft to refreeze, so, help yourself.

BLUNDHILDE. It's not my meat day. Gordon?

GORDON. Yup?

BLUNDHILDE. Phoebe's not in your bedroom, is she?

Beat.

GORDON. Have you seen her?

BLUNDHILDE. I don't go in your room.

GORDON. Where did you see her last?

BLUNDHILDE. Down here, yesterday.

GORDON. Look in the bedroom by all means, and Blundhilde?

BLUNDHILDE. Yes?

GORDON. Let me know if you find her.

Half beat.

CLARENCE. Bad move to have the shower before the drains…

GORDON. Sometimes a man can't sit with his own smell, know what I mean? Joke. I'll be round the side.

He leaves.

BLUNDHILDE. Would you like a mint?

She offers him one.

CLARENCE. Ooh, Fox's Glacier, thanks.

BLUNDHILDE. Have you been in the box room?

CLARENCE. I put the window in there, it's cosy, with that skylight.

BLUNDHILDE. It's basically a cupboard without. Serena told me I couldn't have the guest room because of all the guests but in the eight months since I've been here you're the first to stay.

CLARENCE. They're busy.

BLUNDHILDE. Gordon is.

CLARENCE. He must be late home most nights.

BLUNDHILDE. Those companies rule the world, don't they.

Something in her tone alerts CLARENCE.

CLARENCE. Did you know who Gordon worked for before you got here?

BLUNDHILDE. It was on the form.

Beat.

I'm not allowed pets but yesterday Pepper Anne gave me her hamster to look after.

CLARENCE. An actual hamster?

BLUNDHILDE. He's called Igloo, Iggs for short, he's Siberian. I wondered if you would mind not telling them.

CLARENCE. Right...

BLUNDHILDE. Because Iggs has a thyroid problem so needs exercised twice a day. All you do is get him out his cage and put him in his ball. You don't have to stay, just make sure the door is closed and he goes all over the room, which you know is really small, then after half an hour you put him back in the cage. Could you do that for me, please?

CLARENCE. Let me be honest, is it Brundhilde?

BLUNDHILDE. Blunde, Blundhilde, like blonde.

She has dark hair.

It's not on the Icelandic register, it's just what my mum called me.

CLARENCE. This is a tough one, Blundhilde, because my brother and Serena are trusting me again after some complications in our relationship and, here I am back under their roof, so I wouldn't want to go round breaking their rules, you know?

BLUNDHILDE. Serena says you were a drug addict.

Beat.

CLARENCE. I prefer the word user. I'm making good now, which is a painting term but...

BLUNDHILDE. Like 'making out', or 'make do'.

CLARENCE. Kind of. Basically I've missed out on the last couple of years but I'm in their home again now, you know.

BLUNDHILDE. Sure.

CLARENCE. As it turns out, Rache is away this weekend, which I didn't know she would be.

Half beat.

What will you do with the hamster?

She shrugs.

BLUNDHILDE. I'm going to check for Phoebe.

She goes. CLARENCE *moves his bag and* RACHEL*'s bear out the way. He puts the eggs somewhere safe, then he takes a moment for himself.*

CLARENCE. Dear Higher Power, keep me steady, help make communication between myself and my brother better, please. Keep me on track. May I rise above the wounds, give me patience and perspective, appreciation. Help me earn a place back at their table, make me a worthy uncle. Thank you.

BLUNDHILDE *comes back down with a sheaf of papers, her mood has completely changed.*

She not there?

Beat.

Are you all right, Blundhilde?

BLUNDHILDE. What's wrong with this household where even a hamster, one tiny creature, is too much to look after?

She puts the papers away.

I'm going to Skype Rachel.

Half beat.

CLARENCE. Where's the ball?

BLUNDHILDE. Under the bed.

CLARENCE. Promise me that if you ever get found out you won't grass me up.

BLUNDHILDE. I promise and I don't break promises.

CLARENCE. I'll have to find a time when Gordon's out...

BLUNDHILDE. He smokes.

CLARENCE. He doesn't smoke!

BLUNDHILDE. He does so many things he says he doesn't. I saw him in the garden this morning walking up and down, three cigarettes together. Another thing – do you have a wrench?

CLARENCE. Why?

BLUNDHILDE. To open the toilet tank.

She grabs two bags of rice/quinoa from the kitchen.

Put these inside.

CLARENCE. To save water...? I'm all for rescuing dolphins, green spaces...

BLUNDHILDE. So?

CLARENCE. I'm a recovering alcoholic and drug user, in my brother's home...

BLUNDHILDE. There are no spectators, baby or old man, whatever your problem you cannot not take part, everything you do either saves or cooks the planet.

Beat.

Be sure to put your mint wrapper in the right bin – it's the blue one in the kitchen.

End of Scene.

Scene Two

Saturday night

SERENA *comes home late.*

SERENA. Gordon?

Eventually, he comes from the utility room.

GORDON. Yeah.

He has an empty document sleeve in his hand.

SERENA. What are you doing?

He puts the sleeve out of sight.

GORDON. Looking for Phoebe.

SERENA. Did Blundhilde not find her?

GORDON. No.

SERENA *has a moment of weariness.*

SERENA. I'll look in the morning.

GORDON *is distracted, on edge.*

I had such a good talk with Madeline.

GORDON. Madeline?

SERENA. The trainer.

GORDON. Of course, you said you were going for dinner –

SERENA. She instructs the instructors, she's a really intuitive woman.

GORDON. Great.

SERENA. *So* great.

She sees his open laptop.

I thought you were helping Clarence.

GORDON. Didn't need it.

SERENA. The bolt's still on. And the knob's still off. I felt so brilliant coming home, like I could see everything. Two minutes through the door and I'm deflating like a balloon, headache brewing, complaining again. Come here, you old lump.

She gives him a hug.

Well done on your job.

Beat.

I think it's you who makes me feel rubbish, Gordon. I don't mean it nastily, I just, feel reduced around you.

GORDON. Okay.

SERENA. And your success.

GORDON. Well we should chat about that.

SERENA. *Chat?*

GORDON. Wrong choice of word…

SERENA. I try to say what I feel, you diminish it in a snap, as always.

GORDON. I only meant –

SERENA. You can't pass me on to complaints, Gordon, transfer me to one of your person-centred team…

GORDON. It's late, my head's full.

SERENA. What of – us, our lives, our home? I forgot to ask, did you get the loan?

GORDON. That's what I'm working on.

SERENA. You think we can push through on Monday?

GORDON. Yep.

SERENA. Really?

GORDON. Yep.

SERENA. Where have you gone, I don't know where you are.

Beat.

GORDON. I've been looking for Phoebe.

SERENA. You worried about Rache?

She thinks of her.

Little pigeon…

You're a strange, sweet man.

Half beat.

I had such an amazing day. I felt love for you, proper love, for the first time in ages, I'm sorry if that sounds harsh, I'm just being honest and if we really speak the truth, without revenge or anything mixed with it, it shouldn't be hurtful.

GORDON. Right.

SERENA. That's what Madeline says. At times I've not wanted you anywhere near me in case my disgust would show.

GORDON. Disgust?

SERENA. Or fear that you might give me one of your sucky kisses or rub the veins on the backs of my hands… We don't need to chat, we need to talk and I don't know why that's become so difficult, like we need a fucking appointment to do it. Do you have any cash on you?

GORDON. Yes.

SERENA. Will you just put a twenty in the box for me and have done with it.

GORDON. Can I just say, in case you've not remembered, that Clarence is upstairs?

Half beat.

SERENA. How's the 'bone'?

GORDON. All right, I think.

SERENA. Of course I remembered. I can't remember 'Upon Westminster Bridge' any more, which I used to recite at any social event. Used to be good at English.

GORDON. Sorry, I've a really funny taste in my mouth...

SERENA. And sociable – head of bloody HR, that massive department, had it all sorted!

GORDON. Could have a whisky, it might relax us.

SERENA. Nowadays I flinch when my own daughter calls from upstairs.

Half beat.

I've been balancing all day, Gord, I'm quite relaxed, you're the one that needs to relax.

Half beat.

I'm beginning to wonder if you're a bit fucked.

GORDON *is quiet.*

I mean, I'm fucked too, but at least I know I'm fucked. Did you put that twenty in?

GORDON. No.

He puts a twenty in the swear box.

Don't feel obliged to spend it all at once.

SERENA *finds the perfect name for him.*

SERENA. Sloppy Fucking Giuseppe Gordon.

GORDON. Serena, I'm not in the mood for playing...

SERENA. I'm voicing what's actually in my head.

GORDON. How much did you drink at dinner?

SERENA. I've just come from the most liberating day where I could say whatever I wanted –

GORDON. That's great –

SERENA. And it came out right. I don't like our lives.

GORDON. I know, that's why –

SERENA. Don't cut me off, I don't like our lives and I don't like us in our lives.

Beat.

There are eight minutes at the end of every Balance class where it's relaxation and you can choose to stay or go. Every time, I'm frozen at that juncture – should I stay and unwind and breathe, or should I go, do the shopping? Am I busier and more important if I don't stay, or more evolved and contented if I do? I'm trying to retrain as a calm person because my brain whirrs all the time like that, it doesn't stop.

Beat.

We turned each other's way on the big rotisserie of life and that's very nice and everything but sometimes I wonder if we're good for each other. You used to be more open. Seeing you yesterday with that champagne and those pizzas… it put me in mind of a slug trying to walk, thinking he has legs but he hasn't.

GORDON. I know I'm getting fat.

SERENA. That's not what I meant, who am I to talk?

GORDON. You're not fat.

SERENA. But I starve myself half the day, gym it the other half, it's so effortful. People think money is all it takes, but it's both, effort and money.

GORDON. You're gorgeous…

SERENA. Do you know when I'm at home on Tuesdays and Thursday, I hide in the bedroom when Michaela's cleaning.

Beat.

Having Rache ripped through me and I'm still off kilter. I can't even do Tree on my left leg. Madeline pointed it out today and she's not the first to have said it.

GORDON. These things will get better, Serena.

SERENA. Always smoothing it over – I don't want it smooth, I want it frank. I'm lonely. I don't go out with my old friends any more, it's awkward, I'm too rich, and since she left London I barely even speak to my sister, I had no idea how much I'd miss her, and there you are over there wanting another baby and here I am, terrified of it.

GORDON. It's normal that we're springing a few leaks.

SERENA. I feel I'm hammering at the door of a vacated room. At least I know I'm miserable but I think you'd actually rather die than face things. Honestly, if you could talk about things with me I would live in a tent with you.

GORDON *attends to something unnecessary,* SERENA *watches.*

This displacement activity is exactly what Madeline mentioned.

GORDON. Is Madeline your new therapist?

SERENA. You big infant.

GORDON. It's lucky I'm a confident man, Serena.

SERENA. Just a normal fucking man, you never stoop to asking questions, only when you already know the answer.

GORDON. I'm doing my level best here.

SERENA. I know you work hard, I know, but you say everything's fine when it's not, it's not, Gord, I don't want another child with you!

A small white animal scampers across the room. SERENA *doesn't see it,* GORDON *does. The animal has gone but* SERENA *sees some mess it left elsewhere.*

What's that on the floor, is that – poo?

GORDON. That wasn't there earlier.

SERENA. Have you had the door open? That can't be a cat, can it?

GORDON *rushes to the computer.*

GORDON. The patio door won't close, it's stuck.

SERENA. Stuck? What are you doing?

GORDON. Looking up faeces…

SERENA. What?

GORDON. Fucking touchpad isn't responding…

SERENA. Speak to me, Gordon!

Beat.

Hello, husband not responding…

Half beat.

You admit there are cracks but you're the fucking crack!

GORDON. Okay, I know, there are some areas we need to look at, three areas, or four, let's say five things we need to sort out – shitting computer!

SERENA. Why do you have to take charge, Gordon, you're turning in to a knob-head.

He sees the hamster.

GORDON. There she is!

SERENA. What was it?

GORDON. Shape-shifting little…

SERENA. Where?

GORDON. Yeah.

SERENA. What are you talking about?

GORDON. That… damn…

SERENA. What?

GORDON. Bear.

SERENA. Which bear?

GORDON. The bear. Fucking Phoebe.

The front door closes. BLUNDHILDE *comes in.*

BLUNDHILDE. Hi.

SERENA. Hi, Blundhilde. Gordon just thought he saw an animal run across the hallway, so it's probably best if you leave us to it.

BLUNDHILDE. Was it white?

GORDON. Yes, white!

BLUNDHILDE. About this size?

GORDON. Yes, yes.

SERENA *confronts* BLUNDHILDE.

SERENA. Are you telling me there's something loose in this house?

BLUNDHILDE. That's not what I'm saying, no.

(*To* GORDON.) Where did you think you saw it, as a matter of interest?

GORDON. I don't *think* I saw it, I saw it.

SERENA. What in God's name is going on?

GORDON *continues talking to* BLUNDHILDE.

GORDON. Just there. You've seen her?

BLUNDHILDE. As I told Serena, I've not seen anything.

SERENA. I'm completely lost.

BLUNDHILDE. I'm going to find Clarence, is he upstairs?

SERENA. Yeah.

She goes quickly. SERENA *watches* GORDON.

What are you looking for?

GORDON. Polar bears are very, very clever. 'The strength of twelve men and the wits of eleven'… You mustn't underestimate them, we can't afford to do that.

SERENA. I don't understand what you're saying.

BLUNDHILDE *returns, nips across to the kitchen.*

BLUNDHILDE. Sorry, just need the dustpan and brush, the plant has tipped over, there's earth all over the stairs…

GORDON *hurries to check the stairs.*

SERENA. Help yourself. There's poo on the floor.

BLUNDHILDE. Oh.

SERENA *struggles to understand events.*

SERENA. Something must have got through the patio door...
Gordon seems to think it's a polar bear, in miniature, if I
understand him correctly...

BLUNDHILDE. Would you like me to clear the mess up?

SERENA. That's very kind of you, Blundhilde, very sweet.

BLUNDHILDE. I'll just tidy the soil then I'll come down.

SERENA. Thanks.

BLUNDHILDE *goes off with the dustpan and brush, calling*
CLARENCE.

BLUNDHILDE. Clarence?

SERENA. Look at me, Gordon.

GORDON. Don't worry, I'm going to catch her and show you,
you'll see, you'll see the evil.

SERENA. Gordon. Gordon, will you look at me?

GORDON. You said yourself, it's not cat poo, Serena...

SERENA. Maybe it was a mouse or a rat or something...?

He carries on hunting the creature.

You're scaring me.

CLARENCE *comes running downstairs.*

CLARENCE. Everything okay?

SERENA. Could you talk to your brother please, he's having a
weird turn, which seems to be more comfortable for him
than talking to his wife.

CLARENCE. Gordon?

GORDON *is absorbed.*

I've nearly finished the skirting, Gord. Would you like a cup of Horlicks? Remember how you used to like Horlicks.

SERENA. We don't have any Horlicks...

CLARENCE. Or – (*To* SERENA.) what have you got?

SERENA. Vanilla Chai Latte?

GORDON. They look all fluffy and pure but have you seen a picture of someone mauled by one? They're dangerous, dangerous animals.

CLARENCE. Gordon, I have to tell you that that small animal you just saw – wasn't a bear.

GORDON. I know it didn't *look* like a bear, twat, what do you think I am?

CLARENCE. Mate, it's late, you're tired...

GORDON. Next time she shows herself it'll be in a different form.

CLARENCE *speaks to* SERENA.

CLARENCE. I think we need to find Phoebe as a matter of urgency.

GORDON. Good plan, great plan, first one to find her, come and tell me this isn't all her.

SERENA *starts searching.*

CLARENCE. Gordon...

GORDON. You seen beneath their fur? Dark grey and patchy, like a saggy boar.

SERENA. Clarence, the chai is in a pink pot on the shelf above the kettle.

CLARENCE *goes to the kitchen.* SERENA *tries to take* GORDON *in hand.*

Gordon, you actually have to stop this now, Gordon, stop.

GORDON. They're so cunning and vengeful.

SERENA. You are really freaking me out.

GORDON. Think of the things going wrong – that plant, my glass, the freezer, the water, my charger, the door handle, the patio door, the drains – nothing was blocking them – the dryer – it went off on its own when you were out! And where are my weekend trousers?

SERENA. The dryer was probably on timer…

GORDON. And then I felt it.

SERENA. Felt what?

GORDON. A paw. Touch the back of my neck.

Beat.

And now the goddamn document.

SERENA *is lost for words.* BLUNDHILDE *comes down with the full dustpan and brush.*

BLUNDHILDE. Has Clarence explained?

GORDON *returns to his search.*

GORDON. Come on, you little bastard.

SERENA. Jesus…

CLARENCE *comes out of the kitchen with* GORDON's *chai, he speaks to* BLUNDHILDE.

CLARENCE. I don't know how he got out.

BLUNDHILDE. You must have left the door loose.

CLARENCE. I swear I didn't.

GORDON *is on his hands and knees checking under the sofa.*

BLUNDHILDE. You have to tell them.

SERENA. Tell us what?

BLUNDHILDE. That's not a bear he thinks he's seen.

SERENA. I know it's not, what do you take me for?

CLARENCE. I'll explain, Blundhilde.

GORDON. This is part of it, getting me on my knees where she wants me.

Half beat.

CLARENCE. I'm wondering if we should call someone.

SERENA. It's 1 a.m. Saturday night...

CLARENCE. NHS Direct?

BLUNDHILDE. We could call my mum?

CLARENCE. Has he done this before?

BLUNDHILDE. I mean she's just a nurse, but...

SERENA. Honestly, Blundhilde, feel free to go upstairs, Clarence and I can manage.

BLUNDHILDE *backs off, watches* GORDON. SERENA *speaks to* CLARENCE.

I've never seen him like this. I just came in quite heavy-handed...

CLARENCE. I need to tell you about the bear.

SERENA. What?

CLARENCE. It's a hamster.

GORDON. It may look like a hamster, but it's not. Did you paint that wall? Clarence, have you painted that wall?

CLARENCE. No.

GORDON. See that there?

CLARENCE. Yeah...

GORDON. Serena, Blundhilde?

SERENA/BLUNDHILDE. Yeah.

GORDON. Does that or does that not look like a bear to you?

SERENA. Gordon...

GORDON. Look!

They all peer at the wall.

See? There. Just there, look, the ears. That's the shape of a bear. Who's imagining things now. See it? There you go, exactly, now you've got it.

End of Act.

ACT THREE

Scene One

Sunday afternoon

GORDON *comes warily downstairs*.

CLARENCE. Afternoon.

GORDON. Where's Serena?

CLARENCE. Getting Rache. She took Blundhilde to work the Sat Nav. Can I get you something?

GORDON. Don't treat me like an invalid.

Beat.

CLARENCE. Can you take any time off this week, for the house and stuff?

GORDON. Your tone is fucking unbearable.

Beat.

A hamster was loose in my house and for a moment I mistook it for something, what's so in-valid about that. I am dandy.

CLARENCE. Of course you are.

GORDON. And no I can't take time off, I'm in Germany tomorrow, signing my new contract.

CLARENCE. Well done on your promotion, mate, I've not said.

GORDON. I earn my money, me.

CLARENCE. Doesn't come free for any of us, sadly.

GORDON. I keep the lights on, you paint walls.

CLARENCE. Don't let's argue. I just want to be sure the company's not taking too much from you.

GORDON. If you're feeling sorry for me then you've got the wrong end of the fucking stick, I mean, who are you, Big Daddy Clarence?

Half beat.

Who pays for Mum, Clarence?

CLARENCE. Who visits Mum, Gord?

GORDON. Who has time to visit her? High achievers work and work and then we work some more.

CLARENCE. The big corporations don't always have their employees' best interests at heart.

GORDON. I bring hot water to babies, heat to old ladies and you waft your anti-corporate morals at me.

CLARENCE. I'm not.

GORDON. I manifest the world in people's homes twenty-four seven, what do you do?

CLARENCE. Work six days a week, long hours, skilled work.

GORDON. Then lie back exhausted, let Irene clamber on top at the weekend.

CLARENCE. Why do you mock me? Who's on top in your marriage?

GORDON. Are you judging me, arse-wipe? Put your ancient Irene next to my Serena.

CLARENCE. There'd be no competition, Gord, looks-wise.

GORDON. You've always wanted what I've got.

CLARENCE. That's not true.

GORDON. Coveted my things.

Beat.

CLARENCE. I'll admit, if you met her – Irene has scars, saggy breasts, greasy specs –

GORDON. But to you she's stunning.

CLARENCE. She ribs me, we howl with laughter, she keeps me in recovery. If I hung out with Irene two nights a week for the rest of my days I'd die happy.

GORDON. Is it only two you get?

CLARENCE. She's a busy woman, I'm proud to report.

GORDON. Couldn't afford not to be with a partner like you.

CLARENCE. Can we stop this, can we?

Beat.

I want to say some things.

GORDON. This your five minutes, is it?

CLARENCE. I've not had the opportunity since, your kindness.

GORDON. It was a necessity.

CLARENCE. The kindest thing anyone's ever done, paying for my treatment. And I've undergone changes. I know you don't trust that yet and I understand, because I abused your trust.

Half beat.

The time I came to your house to look after Rachel and you found me taking heroin in the garden.

GORDON. I don't want to hear this.

CLARENCE. And the time I used your telephone to complete my deals.

GORDON. Come on.

CLARENCE. And when I took and sold your video camera, when it had footage of Rachel on it and I didn't know.

GORDON *heads to the kitchen.*

And I abused your trust by befriending Jane.

GORDON *stops.*

Nothing ever happened, I don't blame you for thinking it did but it didn't, I was her friend.

GORDON. That helped her leave her husband.

CLARENCE. Now I'd like to be your friend, if you'll let me.

GORDON. Then you turn up in my second marriage, wreak havoc, till I stop it, then you keep asking us to come and applaud your endeavours as if I had time to sit on plastic chairs and clap.

Half beat.

I earned my way since I was fifteen years old, worked right the way through A levels and uni, while you left and spliffed your way round Europe.

CLARENCE. I don't know how to make it better. Make amends to the brother I admired more than anyone else throughout my childhood. You were everything to me.

Beat.

I'm sorry for being a shit brother.

There is a softening in the air between them. A car pulls up on gravel.

GORDON. See this.

GORDON *holds a piece of paper up for* CLARENCE *to read. It says, 'I MISS YOU RACHEL!'*

Who wrote that?

CLARENCE. Um, didn't Blundhilde Skype Rache yesterday? She was writing stuff from Phoebe…

GORDON. I know you didn't let the hamster out. It was Phoebe manipulating things to make me look cuckoo. No one else sees, but she leaves clues all the time. I went to the toilet, not something you or anyone else would notice, but since yesterday, she's meddled with it.

CLARENCE. Gord…

GORDON. It's flushing differently. So whatever you think, company this, company that, I know what is in fact happening.

CLARENCE. There's a concrete explanation for the toilet sounding different.

GORDON. You wish.

CLARENCE. No, there is.

GORDON. I'm not interested in your theories.

CLARENCE. You actually have to listen to me, what happened yesterday can't happen again, you know, you're a dad. What if Rache were here when you went into that sketch?

GORDON. You can't see it, Clarence.

CLARENCE. Do me a favour, one favour, come upstairs with me and let me show you the toilet. Gord, please, we put some things in the cistern yesterday, Blundhilde and I.

GORDON. Yeah, piss, was it?

CLARENCE. No, no, we put –

GORDON (*cuts him off*). I'm on the level with you and this is what happens.

CLARENCE. Jesus, wait there, stay there, I'm going to go and get the packs, show you.

CLARENCE *runs upstairs*.

GORDON *gets a secret stash of cigarettes out, readies one. He scrutinises the writing on the paper. He gets a Blundhilde note from the fridge, compares the handwriting. It's inconclusive, the lettering is in capitals. He's on his way to smoke outside. Out of the corner of his eye he sees a white figure run into the playroom.* GORDON *turns. He stalks to the door, pulls it closed and draws the lock.*

GORDON. Now I've got you, you little bitch!

He pulls a chair up against the handle.

And I'm not letting you go. You're here till my wife gets home so I can show her who you are, furry fucking demon. Messing with my head. You're severed from my daughter. Before she ever sets eyes on you again, I'm ripping you up, pinning you down, shaving you bald, then I'm going to get a knife…

He goes to the kitchen, gets a knife.

I'm going to get a knife so I can cut your stupid fucking eyes out, plunge my knife inside your brains and cut them off from their stems, roll your sightless dismembered head in shit, foul it with excrement then stuff it down your neck, ex-ex-bear. Give me my fucking document, you cut-wit fuck-shit cunt 'stinct fucker. You're not taking her with you, you're not taking her with you, you're going alone and you're never coming back, wreurrrrghhhhhhhhhhhh!

He is screaming through the door.

The car door slams, CLARENCE *comes running downstairs with the bags from the toilet and a bedraggled Phoebe.* SERENA *rushes in with* BLUNDHILDE, *their arms full of* RACHEL's *luggage.* SERENA *wears a white furry coat,* BLUNDHILDE *wears* RACHEL's *bear ears, the space seems peopled with bears.*

SERENA. What are you doing, where's Rache?

GORDON. Phoebe's in the room, I've got her trapped.

CLARENCE. I've found Phoebe, Gordon, she was under the bath – look.

BLUNDHILDE *tries to alert* GORDON.

BLUNDHILDE. Did you see Rachel? She was in her new outfit, like a little polar bear...

From inside the room, RACHEL's *voice.*

RACHEL (*off*). Mum?

SERENA. Jesus, Rache?

SERENA *runs across, pushes* GORDON. *She speaks to* RACHEL *through the door.*

I'm here, darling, I'm just letting you out. Clarence, take the knife, hold your brother.

SERENA *reassures* RACHEL.

Mummy's here, I'm just here.

Once CLARENCE *has* GORDON, *she unbolts the door revealing* RACHEL, *terrified, in a head-to-foot polar bear outfit.*

It's okay, it's okay, it's okay, it's okay, it's okay.

GORDON *sinks down.*

GORDON. Rachel.

End of Scene.

Scene Two

Sunday evening

GORDON *is on the daybed with a blanket. The mood is utterly changed from the high octane of before.* CLARENCE *and* BLUNDHILDE *watch* GORDON.

Full long beat. When he speaks he speaks quietly.

GORDON. Have you ever seen a hedgehog, Blundhilde?

BLUNDHILDE. No.

GORDON. There used to be thirty-four million on this island. D'you remember the one we found in the park with Dad?

CLARENCE. Yeah.

GORDON. I carried it home. Mum wouldn't let us keep it 'cause of the fleas so we took it back. You ever been to Pompeii?

BLUNDHILDE. No.

CLARENCE. No.

GORDON. Serena and I had a lovely time on Capri when she was pregnant...

Beat.

Pompeii was lively, not Lexuses and laser shows, but you get the feeling they were living. 'When I grow up I'm going to have an electric razor and buy a car magazine each week', that's what I used to want. Not much. We cling on for that. A home, flagon of wine on the porch, cobbled streets and one stone-benched whorehouse. They used to think that that eruption surprised the town but it didn't, they knew it was coming, it rumbled for days, they saw the smoke but they didn't leave. A few elite did, relocate, to homes on the hills. Do you think you'd go, when the alarm sounds, a noise you'd not heard before, would you run through the dark not knowing where you were running to?

Beat.

I can't hear them any more, can you?

He means SERENA *and* RACHEL. *They can't.*

Beat. SERENA *comes out the room.*

SERENA. Asleep.

CLARENCE. Okay?

SERENA. Full of questions. 'Why does Daddy hate Phoebe?'

GORDON. Would you mind putting that light out, Blundhilde – it's glaring at the wall for no reason.

She does.

Are there always this many on?

BLUNDHILDE. Yeah.

SERENA *speaks quietly to* CLARENCE.

SERENA. Everything okay, Clarence, calm?

BLUNDHILDE. My mum could be a really good person to talk to, Serena.

GORDON. I am all right, Serena.

He speaks to CLARENCE.

Do you remember the cameras with cartridge films?

CLARENCE. Yeah.

GORDON. Mum lent me hers for my first school trip, to the Isle of Wight, I was euphoric – what should I photograph, Charlie chucking up on the bus or save them all for the beach? Such decisions, such treasured, blurred results. Rache has thousands of pictures on her iPad mini. She gets so irritated when the thing updates. She'd have liked Mum's camera.

A text comes in on BLUNDHILDE*'s phone.*

In Pompeii they just made those pictures on the walls.

Something bangs against the window, they all jump except for BLUNDHILDE.

SERENA. What the hell was that?

CLARENCE. Blimey.

SERENA. A stick?

Another bang.

Or stone! Not more breaking glass…

Something splats on the pane.

CLARENCE. I might be wrong but that looks like egg to me.

Splat.

GORDON. Two eggs.

Splat.

Three.

SERENA (*to* CLARENCE). You brought eggs.

CLARENCE. Yes, but they're here.

Splat.

GORDON. Four.

SERENA *goes to the door to confront whoever's out there,* BLUNDHILDE *runs to block her.*

BLUNDHILDE. It's my girlfriend.

News to SERENA.

Ex-girlfriend, since yesterday.

Splat, another egg on the window.

GORDON. Five.

Splat.

Six, she's a good shot.

SERENA. Why is your ex-girlfriend throwing eggs at our house?

Another splat on the window.

GORDON. Seven.

SERENA. She'll wake Rachel!

Splat.

GORDON. Eight.

BLUNDHILDE *opens the door.*

BLUNDHILDE. Pepper Anne, stop! Pepper Anne?

There's a short pause, no answer, so she closes the door, then another splat.

GORDON. Nine.

CLARENCE. Are you all right, Gord?

SERENA. You cannot bring your domestics in to our home-life like this!

SERENA *goes to the door again,* BLUNDHILDE *blocks her.*

BLUNDHILDE. It won't work.

Splat.

SERENA. Have you texted or tweeted about the Phoebe incident?

BLUNDHILDE. No, I haven't.

Splat.

GORDON. Eleven.

BLUNDHILDE *throws the door open and shouts.*

BLUNDHILDE. Pepper Anne, give it a break, I mean it, it's not good timing!

SERENA *marches over and shouts out.*

SERENA. Fucking go away, you anarchists!

BLUNDHILDE. One anarchist, one person out there, twenty-three years old.

BLUNDHILDE *closes the door.*

SERENA. What is going on?

BLUNDHILDE. Okay, maybe it's not the best timing, but.

BLUNDHILDE *gets out the papers she hid earlier.*

GORDON. Where did you find that document?

BLUNDHILDE. It was on the bed.

SERENA. Whose bed, our bed?

BLUNDHILDE. Your bag was open.

SERENA. Why did you take something from our room? Oh my god.

BLUNDHILDE. What? What?

SERENA. Have you – ?

BLUNDHILDE. Had sex with Gordon? You are more ridiculous than I thought.

SERENA. What did you just say?

CLARENCE. That was unlikely though, to be fair…

SERENA. Oh, just you tell me I'm ridiculous too, why don't you, Clarence?

GORDON. He's saying I'm ridiculous, not you.

Another egg on the window.

There's the twelfth.

CLARENCE. Let's hope she's vegan.

BLUNDHILDE. She is.

CLARENCE. And stops at two boxes.

BLUNDHILDE *holds the paper.*

BLUNDHILDE. You're my employers and, like, my London family but, this is so much worse than your husband having a stupid affair with anyone.

SERENA. D'you know what, you have undermined me since you damn well stepped into this house, telling me every day how I'm running things the wrong way.

BLUNDHILDE. I didn't mean to undermine you…

SERENA. Then you slip in that you've been in to our bedroom and found a letter and when I remark that that's a bit odd, you insult me. Well, you know what, you can open that door right up again and ask your girlfriend –

CLARENCE. Ex-girlfriend.

SERENA. See if Pepper Anne will bail you out because I don't want you sleeping –

GORDON. Serena –

SERENA. ONE MORE NIGHT UNDER OUR ROOF.

GORDON. Um, hang on…

SERENA. My husband has some kind of episode, terrorises our seven-year-old, my ex-drug-addict brother-in-law is my new best friend because there's no one else around, we have an open house tomorrow with twenty-two viewings booked and she sets her militant ex-girlfriend up to egg our home, then tells me I'm fucking ridiculous.

CLARENCE. Serena…

GORDON. We can't just throw Blundhilde out, Serena.

SERENA. Side with her, why don't you, gentleman? Who smuggled an illegal pet in here, causing some fracture in your mind to gape open like that, who's going to clean her girlfriend's eggs off the windows, and who is in the best position to judge right now whether she should stay or go, me, or you, coming on all coherent.

BLUNDHILDE. Fine.

GORDON. Blundhilde...

BLUNDHILDE. That's fine, I don't care, but I'm not leaving till you've told them what you've done.

She addresses GORDON.

CLARENCE. Easy, Blundhilde.

BLUNDHILDE. What you're doing to Rachel and me and everyone. How much did you pay, five million like they all spend on that shit, or a seat on the board promised to your Secretary of State bitch.

SERENA. Give me that.

SERENA *tries to get the House of Commons-headed paper.*

What do you mean 'doing to Rache'?

BLUNDHILDE. Tell her, tell them.

SERENA. Gordon?

BLUNDHILDE. Or I will.

She starts to read.

'A person has the right to use deep-level land in any way for the purposes of exploiting – '

GORDON *cuts her off.*

GORDON. Okay, all it is, is part of this new bill I've been working on, with the Secretary of State, which the parent company asked for, which means we have to extract UK petroleum and shale gas.

BLUNDHILDE. And sell it for as much as possible, for as long as possible.

SERENA. A bill?

GORDON. So it'll be law. To aid economic recovery, obviously.

SERENA. Right.

BLUNDHILDE. Obviously. Like making your stupid, filthy money is a built-in part of being human or something.

SERENA. Blundhilde.

BLUNDHILDE. He has basically made a document ruining Rachel's future, forcing Britain to pump tonnes of water which there isn't enough of to get new fossil fuels which we don't need to sell and burn and heat the world. Shit. I save everything, the tiniest bit of plastic, I save, I have piles of mint wrappers in my room waiting to come down, I pick toilet rolls out from the upstairs bin. I break my brains working out where to put the lunch box when food is stuck to the sides, do coffee cups go in plastic or paper, what do I do with hardback notebooks when the cardboard has that layer of plastic on, receipts with staples, cling film with sticky labels, kitchen roll, padded envelopes...

She goes to the kitchen, gets the normal bin.

I bet this is full of stuff you've not separated.

SERENA. Don't get the bins out, Blundhilde...

BLUNDHILDE. Look, that's pure plastic, these shouldn't be in here, you have to put them in there!

SERENA. Stop it, Blundhilde, put the bins away.

BLUNDHILDE. I won't stop.

They have an in-out fight over stuff from the bin.
CLARENCE *tries to remind them that they'll wake*
RACHEL.

CLARENCE. Girls, girls, Rachel...

SERENA. Give me that, for God's sake...

BLUNDHILDE. What's this doing here?

SERENA. It came wrapped around flowers, there's metal inside.

BLUNDHILDE. So pull the middle out!

SERENA. Like I'm some kind of elf!

BLUNDHILDE. The borough you're moving to?

SERENA. May be moving to.

BLUNDHILDE. Doesn't collect mixed plastics, so I'm thinking, where will everything go? Like this, or these packs of seaweed, soft packs inside hard plastic inside big wrapping...

SERENA. Problem solved, you won't be coming with us.

BLUNDHILDE. In Switzerland the customers started leaving toothpaste boxes on supermarket floors, that's problem solving!

BLUNDHILDE *finds some pizza in the wrong bin.*

Why's this in here?

SERENA. That's so unhygienic...

BLUNDHILDE. I'm nineteen and I think about this all day long. Hummus pots need hot water to rinse properly but will they recycle it if it's not clean? But what about the petrol for the truck that picks the recycling up...? Do iPads use more energy than paper? Is it better to rinse your cup or put it in the dishwasher? Which waits, on, everything waits, like semi-erect penises everywhere you look in case somebody might want to use something, day or night. I was so excited about coming to London, but you, you –

She addresses GORDON.

Fat, sweaty, white man –

CLARENCE. All right, Blundhilde –

BLUNDHILDE. Are shitting on our lives, you greedy fucking vandal.

SERENA. You cannot speak to your employers that way.

BLUNDHILDE. As you made perfectly clear, Serena, you are not my employers any more.

GORDON *answers gently.*

GORDON. Blundhilde, how did you get here, did you walk, or sail, or thumb a lift with a bird?

BLUNDHILDE. It was my first ever flight.

GORDON. And what fueled that plane, sunlight, was it, steam?

BLUNDHILDE. I loved it. I wish I could be a pilot. I wish I could spend money in Top Shop and fly all over the world, how cool would that be. I wish I didn't carry around bamboo utensils in a recycled pouch.

Another splat at the window.

CLARENCE. She's opened another box.

BLUNDHILDE *throws the door open*.

BLUNDHILDE. Pepper Anne, fuck off and go home, you're a bully. I've just lost my job and I'm telling him, okay, I'm telling him.

She comes back.

In Iceland it's easy to feel the world will go on for ever, with its sunshine which hides its teeth sometimes as clouds sweep over, but it's incorrect.

SERENA. You're not going to save the world with recycling, Blundhilde.

BLUNDHILDE. What am I meant to do? I can't put a windmill on my land because I don't have any land.

GORDON. You know the tower down from the South Bank with those three wind arms up top, know how long they lasted? Three days, then they turned the arms off 'cause every time they went round the floors shook, books fell off shelves, ketchup off tables.

BLUNDHILDE. You expect a baby to walk straight off, then stand and laugh when it falls?

Half beat.

You call shale, 'natural' gas, like ripping up something that has nestled at the centre of the earth since the dinosaurs with such force that it breaks all the ground and means you can set fire to the water –

GORDON. That wasn't us, that was the US –

BLUNDHILDE. Is natural.

GORDON. That tower would be uninhabitable if we'd not stepped in.

BLUNDHILDE. You think living as we live is the only habitable? You and the other companies make so much money from keeping it like that.

GORDON. Come on, Blundhilde, do you blame the kids when their parents make them that way?

BLUNDHILDE. Are you calling yourself a kid, Gordon? You're not, you're a necrophiliac – is that the right word?

CLARENCE. Yeah.

BLUNDHILDE. Screwing a dying world.

SERENA. Christ.

Half beat.

GORDON. You think it's just a matter of a few white blokes deciding to be decent?

BLUNDHILDE. Try it, your kid's bear might stop haunting you.

She goes upstairs.

Beat.

CLARENCE. I'll see if she needs a hand.

GORDON. Not see if your brother does.

CLARENCE. Do you need a hand?

Beat.

CLARENCE *goes upstairs.*

GORDON. Do you mind if I step outside?

SERENA. You mean you want a cigarette.

GORDON *is sheepish.*

Open a window.

GORDON. Pepper Anne might still be there…

Beat.

SERENA. I take it this law is bad for global warming?

GORDON. Yeah.

SERENA. Why's the Government doing it?

GORDON. Money. Shale's abundant and from British soil...
And all their pensions are invested in fossil fuels.

SERENA. Blundhilde might tell the papers.

GORDON. Well, it's their pensions too.

Beat.

I can't believe earlier. I don't know how to...

Half beat.

My sleep's poison. I'm swimming in this river of treacly
stuff, like the bile at the end of diarrhoea, spilling from a
crack in this mountain that I need to try and mend. Rache has
her green spangly goggles on. I try to swim to her but there
are things in my way. She can't see through her goggles. The
things I'm passing are corpses, humans and bears. With
plastic eyes. On the banks, up high, are daisies, tourists
taking pictures and hedgehogs. Then I see Rache is holding
Phoebe, trying to swim. 'Rache!', I yell, 'drop her, let go of
the bear!' She still can't see but Phoebe looks at me. Not
caring if she takes her down.

CLARENCE *carries* BLUNDHILDE*'s suitcase downstairs.*
BLUNDHILDE *brings Iggie in his cage. She goes to the*
playroom.

SERENA. She's sleeping, Blundhilde...

BLUNDHILDE *goes in anyway.*

CLARENCE. I hope you're happy with the way the house is
looking.

SERENA. Sorry, Clarence, I've not even said – it's really smart,
thank you.

CLARENCE. I'm pleased you're pleased. I told Gordon that
this job is my gift to you.

SERENA. Oh, that's very generous...

CLARENCE. It's just the paint. I'd like to be able to offer that too but, if I pick up the tab for that, it capsizes my finances.

GORDON. Knock it off your rehab bill.

SERENA. Gord.

Half beat.

CLARENCE. To be honest, the paint's not even that good. Nice idea being water-based, but there's been no investment in those technologies so you end up having to re-paint every couple of years, fine for us but not so good for the punters, 'specially with kids. They put their hand out to steady themselves and there's a shiny patch for ever.

Quarter beat.

I'm not injecting, I'm not drinking, I'm not smoking, give me a break, I've just chosen a different economic reality to you.

GORDON. Chosen it have you, to not be able to afford the can of paint to dip your brush in.

CLARENCE. I came this weekend hoping for something new, imagining I might even sit down with the family for a piece of toasted cheese or something…

SERENA. Gordon got pizza, did he not say? But a glass broke so –

CLARENCE. It's fine, Serena, honestly – you needed the paint job. I just wonder if you have cash in the house.

SERENA. How much?

He gets the receipt out.

CLARENCE. One four eight for the three pots, including undercoat.

SERENA. Maybe in the swear box…

SERENA goes to the box, empties it. There are plenty of fivers.

CLARENCE. I wouldn't want to take from charity…

SERENA. Let us know if there's a shortfall.

He takes the money. BLUNDHILDE *comes out, picks up Iggie*, CLARENCE *takes her case*.

GORDON. Do you have somewhere to go?

BLUNDHILDE. I'm going to drink merlot and play Clash of Clans with the Australians.

Beat.

For a night or two.

GORDON. Can we call you a taxi?

CLARENCE. I'll take her.

BLUNDHILDE *addresses* SERENA *and* GORDON.

BLUNDHILDE. I don't want to spend one more night under your roof.

SERENA. Look, can I call you tomorrow? It's been a day.

BLUNDHILDE. Rachel can, not you. You stand wringing your hands, 'I'm so unfulfilled, better buy a new top from Sweaty Betty…'

SERENA. How dare you, have you looked at my web history?

BLUNDHILDE. I just take in the parcels – then you go and have a half-hour shower which when you do the sums at the end of life will basically amount to the same as picking up a gun and shooting someone.

SERENA. I have absolutely had it with your revolutionary talk, Blundhilde.

BLUNDHILDE. Me too, boring, huh?

BLUNDHILDE *gives* SERENA *back her house key*.

It's Rachel's first swimming badge on Tuesday, you need to arrive ten minutes early, okay?

SERENA. Okay.

BLUNDHILDE *goes*.

Back to Lewes?

CLARENCE. Shoreham –

SERENA. I mean Shoreham.

He addresses GORDON.

CLARENCE. I'll call to see how you are.

GORDON. Make more amends.

CLARENCE. It's all I can do. I'll send Mum your love. Please tell Rache –

GORDON. Yup.

CLARENCE. That I'd love to see her.

CLARENCE *goes out, the front door slams.*

GORDON. Could you put those last lights out, Serena, would you mind?

SERENA. Let me get some candles first…

She lights candles, eventually turning the last light out.

Are we going to boil in our beds, Gord?

GORDON. No one really knows, but natural disasters will start happening. Have started happening. Droughts won't hit here first – it's more likely to be floods – but it'll mean more people come to the country, poor and hungry – 'cause when you run out of water, you don't die of thirst, you starve. Calais could look like a human chicken farm. And we could get shot on our beaches over a tin of Green Giant.

Beat.

I think shale might be the last nail in the coffin, because we have more shale than time.

We can't run the dirty fuel down any more, won't be forced to or slow our habits.

Beat.

Having the Cabinet in your pocket is not a good feeling, it's that midnight feast when no one tells you to brush your teeth and go to bed. All it really took was, 'Do you want the lights to go out, Minister?'

SERENA. Are you exaggerating about the sweetcorn and the beaches?

GORDON. I don't think so. We get, 'Take fish oil for your joints' – there's hundreds on the market – but not, 'Make your showers too long and you'll make the world unlivable in.'

SERENA. I shower at the gym too. When they say one towel or two, I say two. I dry my hair at the same time as boiling the kettle and watching *Strictly*, I use an electric blanket – how do I hate myself, let me count the ways.

Half beat.

Did you know we're killing the Peruvians by eating so much quinoa, I mean, I don't want to be held responsible for the Peruvians.

GORDON. No.

SERENA. What is it Amazon do or don't do?

GORDON. Tax. Some other stuff.

SERENA. 'I could do with a…', and before I even know it I've bought it. Because it's quick and achievable. Why did I choose this time of all times, to get rich?

GORDON. Even the climate scientists open up their apps and buy a frothy coffee at the weekend.

SERENA. I'm not rich, you are.

GORDON. And I want you to enjoy it.

SERENA. People are up in the air watching episodes of *Humans*, commuting even, but 'cause you work for an energy company and I've had a live-in tyrant dripping this in my ear…

Beat.

Trying to be good ruins my fucking day.

Beat.

GORDON. I am scared for our daughter.

SERENA *holds him, they are the most intimate they've been.*

SERENA. If it's for real, what do we do? I mean, trying to do something about it feels like the boy putting his finger in the dyke, you know, totally hopeless.

Beat.

GORDON. Though that worked.

SERENA. What worked?

GORDON. That boy who put his finger in the dyke, stopped his country from flooding.

SERENA. Did he?

GORDON. He stayed there all night till the grown-ups came, who wrapped him in blankets and fixed the hole.

Beat.

I could pull out.

SERENA. Of CEO?

GORDON. Yeah.

SERENA. You've set the loan up and everything…

GORDON. I've not.

Half beat.

I know I can.

Half beat.

We can't move house without the salary.

SERENA. Course.

Half beat.

GORDON. We'd love it by the river – so long as it didn't flood…

SERENA. We'd save on petrol…

GORDON. We'd save on petrol. But, we don't need to move house.

Half beat.

I'd have to leave the company if I backed out now.

SERENA. Rache would leave her school.

GORDON. I'd get another job. In renewables, even.

SERENA. Would you do that?

GORDON. It's not very sexy.

SERENA. Like hairy German legs.

GORDON. Needs a makeover, but they actually know how to do it, just needs investment. Once it's up it's peanuts to run – sun, wind, tides.

SERENA. What would it cost UK to go hairy?

GORDON. A hundred and ten billion.

Beat.

Hard to walk from the fortune that's sitting in the ground and pay that much for the pleasure.

SERENA. I'd have to work out who to be, the wife of a green-energy frontman. I couldn't fly and see my family… but I'm behind you, Gord, if that's what's doing you in, of course…

Half beat.

We could move to Shoreham, keep chickens.

There is affection and humour between them.

How much good would it do, if you put a halt to that bill?

GORDON. It could make a worldwide splash. I'd be going against Government, parent company, the already nervous shareholders… It might inspire China. They're on the case, but to step down when you've only just got to the front of the queue, oh cool, yeah, we'll have one phone instead of three, catch a train, take one for the team…

Beat.

Customers are up for it.

SERENA. Not the climate deniers.

GORDON. Tiny minority.

SERENA. Vehement though!

GORDON. I can't pretend we've not been glad of them.

Beat.

SERENA. If the likes of you stand up and say we're in trouble, people would believe you, wouldn't they.

GORDON. For once.

Beat.

SERENA. When Rache says she wants the lights on 'cause she's scared at night, we'd have to say, 'No darling, 'cause if you keep the lights on what's coming will be an awful lot scarier.'

GORDON. If the world could tell its children at the same moment…

SERENA. They do learn about it at school.

GORDON. Make the last mindless Google search, eat the last daily burger, drop our wages, together. Because unilateral doesn't work. *If you're not doing anything about it, why should I?*

SERENA. How do you organise multilateral, worldwide, self-denial…?

Half beat.

GORDON. Our industry could lead. If we gave up getting stuff out the ground, people would stop buying.

SERENA. Who of the Big Six would do that?

GORDON. There's the rub, who's ready to admit they're a dinosaur?

SERENA. You're not a dinosaur to me.

GORDON. D'you know the sediment left over from humans will settle on the earth's crust like a cigarette paper, that's how thin it'll be. All this huffing and puffing and human life amounts to a parenthesis.

Beat.

SERENA. Can't believe I'm saying this but, what if it's just evolution? It was nice having some warm weather this summer…

GORDON. Serena.

SERENA. Just playing devil's advocate. I mean, on a depressed day, who are we humans anyway?

GORDON. If you asked those bodies from Pompeii if they had their time again, would they choose to stay or would they listen to the alarm bells and run, what would they say?

Beat.

Fifty years' time, Rache'll only be fifty-seven.

Beat.

SERENA. Gord, I'm on the pill.

GORDON. Since when?

SERENA. Few months. I get so overwhelmed. I think I've basically been depressed since Blundhilde's been here.

Beat.

I can't live with imagining this stuff. Even keeping the reality of it in my head, it's so mammoth, horrifying.

Half beat.

But the fact that you're saying these things, thinking them, I love that. This was locked up in you.

Half beat.

Some monster could come in and become CEO instead of you and make it all even worse, then what would we do? At least if it's you we know there's a good man in the role.

GORDON. I don't know how good a man I am.

SERENA. Look at me, that guilt does you no good, you're a good man. There are so many people doing such wicked things, it's insane that you're the one that gets eggs pitched at you.

GORDON. We used to be hailed as magicians, bringing supplies to all corners of the earth.

Half beat.

I'm glad I know about the pill.

SERENA. I should have told you.

GORDON. She's such a blessing, our girl.

Beat.

Doesn't giggle as much as she used to, does she.

SERENA. It's a lot of driving at the moment.

Beat.

If climate disaster is honestly going to happen in Rachel's lifetime, the reality is she's going to need one hell of a nest egg, isn't she? I had such a shit education. I want Rache coming out smart from that school, finding a place at the top table…

GORDON. Able to protect herself.

Double beat.

Do they have a rifle range in Bushy Park?

SERENA. Why?

GORDON. Let's find out. Book her some lessons.

The noise of the tumble dryer starts up.

SERENA. Is that the…? That timer must be faulty.

She goes to investigate.

Beat.

The computer comes on by itself – SERENA*'s Balance class,* GORDON *stops it. A final solo egg flies against the window.* RACHEL *appears from her bedroom in her polar-bear outfit and* BLUNDHILDE*'s bear ears.*

GORDON. Hello, Rache.

Beat.

I'm so sorry about earlier... Daddy wasn't at all himself.

Beat.

We should get you out your suit and into your pyjamas.

Beat.

RACHEL. It's dark.

GORDON. Isn't it.

Beat.

Do you like the candles? Look at the shadows!

Double beat.

RACHEL. Can we switch the lights on?

SERENA *watches from the doorway.*

Beat.

End.

A Nick Hern Book

Fuck the Polar Bears first published in Great Britain in 2015 as a paperback original by Nick Hern Books Limited, The Glasshouse, 49a Goldhawk Road, London W12 8QP, in association with the Bush Theatre, London

Fuck the Polar Bears copyright © 2015 Tanya Ronder

Tanya Ronder has asserted her moral right to be identified as the author of this work

Cover photograph by Eric Richmond; design by Well Made

Designed and typeset by Nick Hern Books, London
Printed in Great Britain by CPI Group (UK) Ltd

A CIP catalogue record for this book is available from the British Library

ISBN 978 1 84842 510 1

MIX
Paper from
responsible sources
FSC® C013604
www.fsc.org